STATE OF MAINE
DEPARTMENT OF HUMOR

JOSEPH E. BRENNAN
GOVERNOR

To: Lance Tapley, Publisher
      86 Winthrop Street
      Augusta, ME   04330

Dear Mr. Tapley:

Be advised that the Maine Department of Humor regulates any effort at publishing, uttering, or even thinking about the subject of "Maine Humor." According to our regulations, such humor efforts must contain:

A. 50% Biblical-sounding names for characters.

B. 50% of references to towns must refer to towns with population under 1,000.

C. At least one reference to a dead Republican President.

D. A minimum of 25% of the humor must refer to some form of fishing.

E. Maine natives must be portrayed as possessing freeze-dried wits.

F. At least one person involved in the project must be from out-of-state, but have a Maine accent.

I'll be flying in from Aroostook County later this week so my arms will be too tired to turn the pages of your manuscript at that time (ha-ha), but if you have any questions, contact my office. Good luck on your project. From what I hear of the Wicked Good Band, you are going to need it.

Very truly yours,

Bert N. Eye
Commissioner

The Wicked Good Book

Steve Bither
& the Wicked Good Band

Lance Tapley, Publisher

Cover design and illustrations by George Hughes. Text design by Type & Design, Brunswick, Maine.

Printed in the United States of America.

Library of Congress Cataloging-in-Publication Data

Bither, Steve, 1948-
  The Wicked Good book.

  1. Maine — Anecdotes, facetiae, satire, etc.
I. Title.
PN6231.M18B58   1985   947.1'00207   85-25013
ISBN 0-912769-04-1

For Patricia, Elise, Lynda, Nancy, Ben, Hannah, Jonah.
For Cliff Rugg: Thanks for the piano.
For Rufus Dufus & the Duffers: Your memory lives on.

CONTENTS

CONTENTS

*We can make your house look like this on the
outside ...*

1. DARE TO BE WICKED GOOD
(Lifestyle Conversion Kit)

Everyone in Maine is trying to make a little money. But it seems the only people in Maine that are making any money are the people who sell things that exploit Maine, or those darn Yuppies. So The Wicked Good Band got together and figured out a way to make money ourselves from people "from away" while we taught the Yuppies a thing or two about our state.

We developed a program called "Dare to be Wicked Good." It's a $199.95 lifestyle conversion kit that can make the slickest New Yorker into a real Maineiac. You'll see some of the program material throughout the book. The course covers everything, such as:

• How to make your Halston dress look like a polyester pantsuit.

• How to make your exposed-brick apartment look like the inside of a ten-foot-wide trailer.

• How to make a gourmet meal look and taste like a church-supper casserole.

But the most important part of the whole thing is your car. Have you ever seen a shiny new car on the road in Maine? There's a good chance this car is from away. If the car itself isn't from away, a Maine person will think that the driver must be. In fact, some towns, those more than ten miles away from Route One, have considered banning such cars as subversive foreign elements. There are some bean suppers in the state which will refuse service to a person who has a car that looks too nice.

This is where the Dare to be Wicked Good (DTBWG) Automotive Kit comes in. We can make your car look like it is from Maine; as a result, you could be mistaken for a true Mainer yourself.

Let's start with the grill. Now it might be okay to have a flashy grill on trendy Exchange Street in Port-land, but in the Real Maine it just won't do. The DTBWG Automotive Kit has a replacement grill, so no matter what kind of car you started out with you end up with something that looks like a 1974 Plymouth.

If you can see the reflection in the shine of your car, it won't qualify for being Wicked Good. The DTBWG Kit contains a can of Mr. Rotto Rust Starter. Just spray it around the rocker panels, the headlights, anywhere that has no rust but should have. And you can add years of wear to the paint job by using the Official Seal of Maine: Bondo. Slap on about ten pounds of Bondo and make little twirls in the top, just like they do at the Dairy Joy. Having Bondo on your car is a sign that you have faced up to

Be sure to get that Rust Starter around the headlights.

the challenge of Maine roads and Maine winters — and that you've lost the challenge.

You've got the major part of the outside done. For a finishing touch, spray just a couple of drops of our Eau de Skunk around the tires and decorate under the front bumper with some raccoon hairs. For the back bumper, be careful of what your sticker says. A person in a Peugeot with "El Salvador is Spanish for Viet Nam" disappeared in Dover-Foxcroft. Try something a little more Maine-like. We provide your choice of "Nuclear Power Plants Are Built Better Than Jane Fonda" or "I Speed Up for Small Animals."

Now you have done a pretty good job with the appearance. It's time for a little suspension work. Each DTBWG Kit contains a sledgehammer. Muckle onto it and give a whack to the suspension system, either the right or the left side. Bash out the shocks for a pothole-type ride even on new pavement. It's got to tilt to one side a bit. A car that sits even on the road has to have been travelling down too many straight and narrow paths.

Next for the interior. In order to get that lived-in, driven-in smell, get a couple of six packs of Old Lewiston Beer, drink 'em down, and throw the empties on the floor. Not only will this add ambiance, but you can try to use the returnables to pay the tolls on the Turnpike.

Appearances aren't everything. You've got to have the right type of registration and inspection. Follow our accompanying photo article for how to inspect your own car the Wicked Good way. The sticker you get from this inspection will be good for a couple of months, by which time your car will be ready for the junk heap anyway.

Finally, to make your car run as if it had always been in Maine, we recommend Presumpscot Motor Oil. This fine, 200-weight, antidetergent oil should be poured directly into your gas tank to give your car a beautiful blue exhaust. Then people can tell when you're coming, or where you've been. And what a fine aroma! Now just let a little air out of the semibald retread tires we supply, and you're ready to roll.

WICKED GOOD CAR INSPECTION TIPS

When you have a piece of junk for a car, there's always the problem of government regulation. Inspection stickers are required to be renewed once a year, but the mechanics at inspection stations put the car through such rigorous tests, like seeing if the brakes work, that hardly anybody passes the first time. If you don't have the twenty bucks to pay the mechanic for a "special" inspection sticker (where he inspects the twenty and gives you the sticker), then you need simple instructions to do your own car inspection at home.

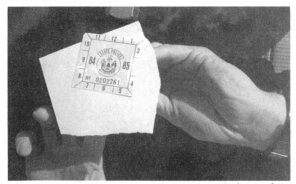

CHECK THE COLOR of the sticker and match it using a watercolor set. Thoroughly color a piece of paper in the matching tint.

INSPECT THE WINDSHIELD from the inside to make sure the color is a good match.

CHECK THE MONTH and make sure you have written the right number to match the hole you are covering.

CHOOSE ANOTHER MONTH to cut another hole out of with knife or razor blade. Don't forget to make it a month that comes after the month you're replacing!

THE FINAL PRODUCT. The State Police will never know it's a "do your own" job.

ARE THEY WICKED GOOD?

We asked a Panel of Experts about some automotive aspects of Maine life.

CORVETTE STING RAYS

yes	no	
☐	☑	Rust-proof body. Hard to apply Bondo.

LICENSE PLATES

yes	no	
☑	☑	Plates with low numbers — yes. Vanity plates — no.

CARS WITH FINS

yes	no	
☑	☐	The whole country started going downhill when they took those fins off.

CARS WITH INTERNATIONAL STICKERS OF ORIGIN

yes	no	
☐	☑	Are you kidding?

"Harry, are we Wicked Good?"

2. FROM AWAY

CAN SOMEONE WHO IS FROM AWAY BE WICKED GOOD?

The term *from away* is used, only half in jest, by xenophobic* Mainers who think that being from Maine bestows an air of authority about something. Just like the different types of vegetarianisms, there are varying degrees of being from away. It is generally accepted that one who moved to Maine during his or her adult life is from away. But what about those who come to Maine as children? If you graduate from a Maine high school, say in a place such as Madison, some Maine-ness can be inculcated, and you can only be regarded as seventy-five percent from away. If you started kindergarten in Maine and went all the way through school here, you get rated forty percent from away. If you were born in, say, Massachusetts and moved to Maine at age six months, you will still be regarded as twenty-five percent from away. If, before you were born, your parents were from away, there is still a hard-core ten percent of people who will hold this against you. If your ancestors were in Maine before 1600, most Mainers will conveniently forget the fact that *their* ancestors came from away and took the land from your ancestors.

We in the Wicked Good Band are not from away, but we don't think there's anything special to being from Maine. Some of the biggest jerks we have known have come from Maine. Of course, some even bigger jerks we have known have come from away.

A person who comes into Maine to live may not realize it, but longtime Mainers have a way of recognizing how long someone has been a part of the state. The Maine Department of Heritage Haberdashery has issued these clothing guidelines to differentiate the various classes of Mainers.

Class I: Lived in Maine under ten years or first-generation Maine resident: L.L. Bean boots for men, L.L. Bean rubber-top ankle boots for women.

Class II: Eleven to thirty years in Maine or parents are less than fifty percent from away: L.L. Bean boots which have been resoled or which

*Look it up.

have new uppers. For the women, Elvis sweatshirts.

Class III: (for many, this is the acid test of whether one is from away): Third-generation Mainer or over thirty years full-time (and no more than two weeks at a time outside the state, even Florida): The official Milton M. Young-model red-and-black-checked cap, in wool with flannel lining. One size fits all. Women have the option of wearing the hat or mukluks. (Note: see Milton M. Young section later.)

The hat

Class IV: The Department will issue to any Mainer who is *both* over age fifty and who is at least a fourth-generation Mainer a matching pair of green Dickies pants and green Dickies work shirt. This is the highest order of achievement, and, when it is worn with the Milton M. Young red-and-black-checked hat, you have the right to be as crusty and narrow-minded as you wish. For the ladies, a red BVD union suit and costume jewelry made with Maine rhinestones and purple glass signify the same.

Now, if you are classified as being from away and you want to be Wicked Good, here are some do's and dont's:

DON'T SAY: "Well, my uncles and aunts all summered here, so that's almost the same as being a real Maine person."

DO SAY: "I remember working on the Horace Hildreth for Governor campaign and all those bean suppers we put on."

DON'T SAY: "I'd like to buy one of those big old houses in a little coastal town and maybe settle down and practice law."

DO SAY: "I can't wait to get out of this old, drafty, hard-to-heat house and move into an all-electric ranch in a development near Portland, so I don't have to see relatives or people I owe money to every time I turn around."

DON'T SAY: "Ayuh," "Finestkind," or "chimbley," if you are from away. You can't say it authentically, no matter how hard you try.

DO: Liberally sprinkle your talk with "wicked" as a substitute for "very," and "frig" as a substitute for...well, about anything that requires it.

If you're from away, in short, don't try to hide it, but don't make big deal out of it. Just because the chances of a person from away becoming Wicked Good are about the same as putting a skidder through the eye of a needle, don't be upset. There are things you *can* do:

- Become a good candlepin bowler.
- Have a cottage at the lake, and let it be known that you like company and they can go water skiing any time.
- Throw your own yard sale and sell more atrocious junk than they do.
- Fix lawn mowers, chain saws, and snowmobiles.

If all else fails, you'll need the Wicked Good Indoctrination Course, the primary feature of which consists of forty days and forty nights in the Desert of Maine. Next is an excerpt from one pilgrim's diary, as found in the basket at the Kittery toll booth...

Put one of these in your back yard. No one will suspect you're from away.

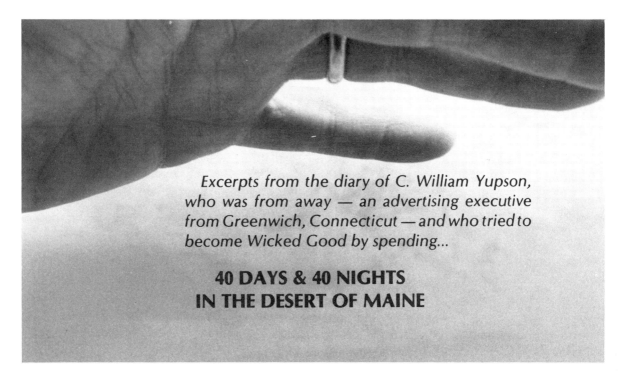

Excerpts from the diary of C. William Yupson, who was from away — an advertising executive from Greenwich, Connecticut — and who tried to become Wicked Good by spending...

40 DAYS & 40 NIGHTS
IN THE DESERT OF MAINE

Day 1: I see the hot sun glimmering off the top of the Volvo. I see the Toblerone I bought for energy melting on the front seat. But I cannot go back. This is a more important quest for me than landing the Tudbury account. If I can't be Wicked Good I don't think there's much worth living for. I trudge off to find my destiny...

Night 3: The stars have again formed a giant bowl overhead. Although I hear the traffic on Route One, I am developing my own Route to Maine One-ness. Tonight I drank my first Moxie. I thought the bitter taste had something to do with my canteen, but I had been warned: First the bitterness of Moxie, then the sweetness of Wicked Good...

Day 6: All day when I look at the little pit of sand next to this oak tree, I think of golf. I want to use a

sand wedge and blast out onto the green. But there is no green. There is only the sand, and the wind, and the sun burning down. I thought I saw a red-and-black-checked cap near the snack bar today. This must be a sign that I can succeed...

Day 12: Day visitors swarm the place, crawling like locusts. I loath them and their Winnebagos and their Hawaiian shirts. I want to throttle them when they whine about the crabmeat rolls at the snack bar. I want to shout at them that they are invading my space, that they wouldn't know a Wicked Good if it crawled into bed with them and made disgusting noises all night. I suppress my anger as I slouch off behind the tree I have adopted. Behind the tree I find my next instruction, the consummation of a case of Narragansett...

Night 16: Two more bottles of Narraganset to go, and I fear I have not developed a liking for it any more than I could for Moxie. Doubt seeps in, and sadness, with the realization that many are from away, but few are Wicked Good...

Day 20: In my old life, if I were to sell a million dollars of useless face cream to thousands of people, it would have been an ordinary event. But today was special! I took a small cache of seagull poop, wrapped it in a plastic bag, labelled it "Seagull Poop," and sold it to an out-of-stater for a dollar and a half! I never felt such exhilaration as I did when I took that money from that stupid tourist. A voice seemed to be saying to me in the middle of the sunny day: "Anything to make money!"

Night 20: Beans! Beans! Beans! Will these infernal beans never stop! For the past two weeks, the Wicked Good Program has left a box under the tree just before dinnertime. The box, marked "Bean Supper to Go," contains a complete bean supper from a Maine church. My job is to detect which denomination. I am getting better at it. Last night I was able to detect Lutheran, but tonight I couldn't even get a good guess. I didn't know that Christian Scientists even had bean suppers! For once, I am thankful for the wide-open spaces of the desert...

Day 28: The "desert" experience becomes very strange when it is raining. Rain has been incessant for the past four days. The red-and-black-check-ered-hat man walked right by me today, and his pipe was still smoking in the rain. His serene gaze made me wonder what was in that pipe, anyway. I had my pork-pie hat on. The checkered-hat man looked squarely at me, and I felt he was reading my soul: "You are a faker," he seemed to say, "and I can tell by that hat." But all he said was: "Good weather for ducks, ain't it?" What could be the significance of that? Is it a quaint Maine saying? I never heard that on *Bert and I* ...

Night 32: It's finally stopped raining, but I wish I could have some of the rain back instead of this frost. My down sleeping bag had about a half-inch of frost on top of it this morning, and, as I trudged on my visit to the outhouse, I felt an intense Maine flash: wicked boredom. My task was thus laid before me for the next eight days, and — if I want to continue — for the rest of a possible Wicked Good life: withstand the boredom and fight off the cold and the bugs and the rain. I'd rather have to hustle a hundred new accounts. But the thought of my children's children's children being able to wear that red-and-black-checked cap keeps me here...

Day 35: It's hotter than any other day has been so far. Mirages abound. I look for camels and in fact see them. It's the old man in the red cap, looking at me and offering a Camel. "Goin' through the course, are ya?" he asks. "Ayuh," I say, on the intake of breath. I don't think it sounds too bad. But his eyes flash with anger, then crinkle back into a smile. "It's a long battle, and it ain't over till the last day," he said conspiratorially, and then walked away. I have never felt so alone, so unsure, so un-Wicked Good as when he disappeared. Was he the tester, and was I failing? Or was I being prepared for the last day?

Night 38: I hadn't seen my car since the first day, but I thought I would go a bit closer to see if it was all right. At first, I had trouble finding it in the dark underneath those pines. And then, when I saw it, I couldn't believe it was the same car. It was dotted with rust. The front grill had been removed and replaced with an old Plymouth grill. And where there once had been melted Toblerone, there was a pine-tree-shaped air freshener. I looked in the back seat and saw back issues of hunting magazines and empty beer cans of three or four different types of beer. Someone had to have been in this car! I nearly forgot about the quest as I angrily left the desert and headed into town to find the police.

It looked like a quaint-enough town, but all the stores were closed. Except for a large department-type store. I now realized it was three in the morning. But there were still dozens of Volvos, just like mine used to be, in the parking lot. And there were a hundred shoppers in the store, buying up clothing that I once thought was necessary to own, but tonight felt no need for. As I turned to leave, I spotted a small flash of red at a table out of the mainstream of traffic. I went to the table and there I found...a red-and-black-checked hat! I tried it on. It was a bit tight, but when I pulled the flaps over my ears it felt perfect. As I turned to find a mirror, I bumped into the old man, who was wearing a pair of green Dickies pants and shirt. "You like it?" he asked. "Ayuh," I said, just a tad off on the intake. The man snatched it off my head and with anger said: "You're not ready for it yet!" Before I could recover from my shock he was gone, and I was back out in the street, headed for the desert, having forgotten about the police.

I hitchhiked a ride back with a guy in an old Pontiac — about a '73 — with a clear view of the road below from his front seat. He told me his car had been a BMW before he took "the course." "But why are you still here?" I had to ask. "Because it's here," he said, but wouldn't elaborate.

I returned at daybreak, more confused than I had ever felt. I am sitting here finishing off another case of Narragansett under the tree, and I think I'm ready to take a nap, now that it's close to noon...

Day 40: I wake at daybreak after sleeping fitfully. In my dreams were plastic flamingoes and big plastic butterflies, all marching around a gigantic wooden statue shaped like the state of Maine, and inside the statue the old man with the twinkling eyes

looked right through me as he said: "You'll always be from away. Why don't you give up now?" The rest of the desert is deserted. The snack bar is closed. No obnoxious tourists are here. I trudge toward my car to find if it really looks as bad as it seemed the other night. But when I get to the parking lot, I am greeted by the officials from Wicked Good, Inc.! They are noncommittal as they hand me my diploma, my L.L. Bean-type boots that aren't from L.L. Bean, the three free strings of candlepin bowling, the year's pass into any bean supper. They are telling me I am Wicked Good! But their attitude is far from the Academy Awards.

"What's the matter, did I do something wrong?" I ask.

"No," the apparent leader of the group tells me. "You're Wicked Good. You've got a paper that says you're Wicked Good, and you've got the paraphernalia that means you're Wicked Good."

"But..." I say.

"But, you'll probably leave Maine, and next month you'll sign up for EST, or you'll buy a Preppy Handbook, and then this Wicked Good stuff will all be part of your past. It won't have any lasting meaning."

"No," I tell them. "At first, I really wanted to be Wicked Good. Then I felt like I was there. Now I don't particularly give a shit whether I am or not, but I know I'm not gonna go for another program. I don't need a program to know what I know."

"Did you say you don't give a shit?"

"That's right. Even about the car rotting away." The leader gives me a long, hard look. Then he

says: "Take a look in this mirror."

So I do. Yeah, I see I only have half as many teeth as when I started. Big Deal..."I am wicked hungry after being out here so long. I could really go for a casserole," I say.

They all look at each other and nod their heads. From their midst, the old man appears, actually smiling this time. He puts the red-and-black-checkered hat on me. "You're Wicked Good now, son," he says.

"Ayuh," I tell him, the wind whistling through my teeth.

"But you're still treading on thin ice when you say that," he says with a laugh.

Night 40: It is hard to leave the place where I've gone through so many changes, but I've got to get out and do my part. The wife is going to be surprised to see the skidder on the streets of Greenwich, but she'll have to get used to it. Tudbury is going to have to get used to my wearing the red-and-black-checked hat when I chase down their account. But if they don't adapt...who gives a shit? I'm leaving this diary at the toll booth for the next person who tries the Wicked Good course. Some may fail, but there is always the hope that a new hat will be issued and the world will be enriched by one more convert who came "from away" and returned Wicked Good.

THE STORY OF THE FIRST WINNEBAGO

THERE'S ALWAYS BEEN SOMEONE WHO HAS BEEN "FROM AWAY"

(Excerpt from the Diary of Squire Josiah Cranbrook, a Gentleman from New Jersey)

THE WIFFE liketh not travell by shippe, yet she expressed a desire to view the Province called Main. For such an journey and in such uncouthe an terraine, I instructed my servants to construct a suitable means of conveyance for both travelling and for protection from unpleasant heathen elements.

The vessell thence constructed, for vessell it was, surpassed all dreams of magnificence. It was more a shippe on wheels than a rude carriage. Inside, one found those comforts usually associated with one's own hearth. A chimney on one end and a small black pot over the fire place. Bundles of straw for sleeping in — to avoid the fleabitten local innes we were sure to encounter, And, wonder of wonders, a built-in chamber potte. Upon completing one's duties, one need only lifte a small handle and the pot's contents are distributed on the road below...

Some People Will Always Be From Away

(From the word processor of
Mr. and Mrs. Bob & Wendy Yurtbrick-Weiner)

Dear Publisher,

I object to the depiction of all people as skidder-driving, lawn-ornament-collecting, candlepin bowlers that you have allowed in this presophomoric text you call The Wicked Good Book.

My husband and I have lived in the grand state of Maine for more than three years now and consider ourselves to be quite the "Mainers," and we have never even seen a skidder, no less drive one. As for lawn ornaments, we think they are the tackiest, most inappropriate "ornaments" a beautiful state like Maine could possibly have. Needless to say, the only bowling we have ever done was years ago and that was with the traditional duckpins.

You would do well to publish literature that promotes the upscale side of the state of Maine. Why not present a witty portrait of the new Mainers, those professionals who are bringing a new vitality and sense of aesthetic wonder to a state which, let's face it, has become quite stale, cerebrally speaking?

Instead of propagating the myth of the Maine hick, why not present Maine the way it really is: reinvigorated!

Yours Truly,

Mr. and Mrs. Bob & Wendy Yurtbrick-Weiner

LANCE TAPLEY, PUBLISHER

86 WINTHROP ST. • P.O. BOX 2439 • AUGUSTA, MAINE 04330 • (207) 622-1179

Dear Readers:

As the publisher of this book, let me say that it has always been my intent to please "new" Mainers as well as the old. The remarks of the Yurtbrick-Weiners are well taken. And so, in an effort to present the best side of the new Maine, I have asked the authors of this book to present the following profiles of upscale Mainers.

Sit back, kick off those L.L. Bean loafers, crack open a bottle of Poland Spring Water to wash that croissant down, and, most of all, enjoy.

Sincerely,

Lance Tapley
Publisher

LT/jr

Mainely Business

Business Profiles of People Who Move to Maine to Bring a New Sense of Wonder to the State, Aesthetically Speaking, and to Make a Lot of Money from the Hicks and Tourists

EDITOR'S CORNER

We dedicate the following piece to the lobbyists at the state capitol in Portland. The hallways and cloakrooms of the capitol building are abuzz with a new kind of political action from a new kind of political activist ... the lobbyist. Let the duffers in their leisure suits sit in their seats in the legislature and think that they're running the state. We'll discover that it's the lobbyist who really pulls the strings in the lobbies of Portland.

MEET LAWRENCE MALOY — Lawrence Maloy is prowling the halls and lobbies of the state capitol in Portland. It's a typical day for Maloy. Dressed in a peach-colored, natural-look, three-piece suit from Armani, Larry looks as good in a high-pressure business meeting as he does at the after-session parties where he meets with other lobbyists to conduct the real business of the state of Maine and drink scotch.

Today, Maloy is pressing the flesh of legislators to garner support for a bill to increase the deposit on all returnable bottles and cans. Larry is wearing classic black-tassle loafers from Cole-Hahn. Whether he's giving testimony or dancing the latest dance steps at his favorite Portland disco, his feet will always be in fashion.

Larry, whose law practice is in the suburbs of Portland, our capital city, is lobbyist for the Maine People Who Collect Returnable Bottles Association. He drives a classic 1973 Caterpillar skidder through the woods around his lawn-ornament-bespeckled trailer or when he goes candlepin bowling on Saturday ...

Dear Publisher,

We object to the general direction this piece of alleged humor seems to be taking. Once again, you have chosen to depict the typical Mainer as a real hick.

While it started out appropriately enough, the authors once again saw fit to drift into their typical, degrading portrait of the Maine person as a second-class citizen.

We believe you should force these "authors" to write something of redeeming social value. By the way, do you really expect us to believe that someone would wear black-tassle loafers with a peach-colored Armani suit? Ha, ha, ha!

Sincerely,

Mr. and Mrs. Bob & Wendy Yurtbrick-Weiner

MEET PAT PEACH — Pat Peach is the best Portland has to offer. Sophisticated, well-educated, she works for a Portland brokerage firm. She doesn't watch television except for Dick Cavett reruns.

Ms. Peach spends a good deal of time in the Forest City's capitol hallways and cloakrooms, protecting the interests of her brokerage firm and not watching television.

Ask any of the legislators who know this feminine-yet-tough-minded politico and they'll tell you that they've never seen her watching television. Rep. Louis Gallblad (R-Lewiston) said: "She doesn't even watch the monitor when the local news crews are here filming a story. I tell you, eh, she may be a woman but she doesn't watch television!"

Here's Ms. Peach in her fine, exposed-brick office on Exchange Street in Portland. She specializes in surplus cheese futures for her brokerage firm. "I get a good deal of satisfaction from having the social safety net land wealth and riches for my clients," she said.

And what does she do in her free time? Well, when she has free time, and that's not often, she enjoys collecting pink flamingoes and other lawn ornaments to display around her Portland townhouse. She and her husband, Wilfred, a Portland attorney, spend a good deal of their free time in the basement of their Portland townhouse exploding skidder tires to stuff with plastic marigolds, as well as spinning daisies which they sell during their weekly yard sale in front of their Portland townhouse. "It's just something we ...

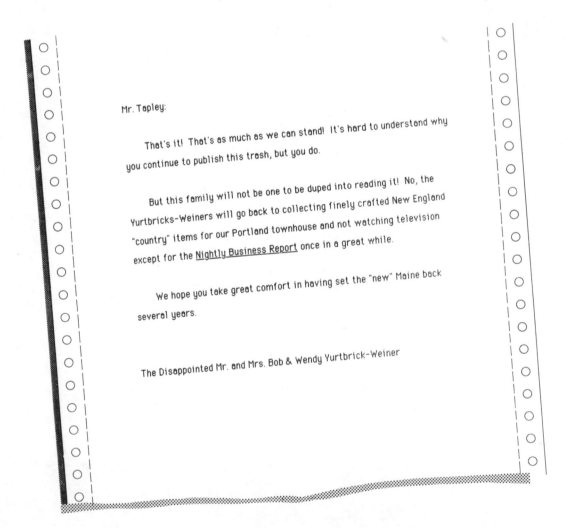

Mr. Tapley:

That's it! That's as much as we can stand! It's hard to understand why you continue to publish this trash, but you do.

But this family will not be one to be duped into reading it! No, the Yurtbricks-Weiners will go back to collecting finely crafted New England "country" items for our Portland townhouse and not watching television except for the Nightly Business Report once in a great while.

We hope you take great comfort in having set the "new" Maine back several years.

The Disappointed Mr. and Mrs. Bob & Wendy Yurtbrick-Weiner

3. WICKED GOOD HUMOR

Living in Maine is a lot of laughs. Where else can you find thousands of rusted-out cars with license plates advertising Vacationland? Where else do spruce budworms proliferate on fir trees? Face it: in order to survive in Maine you have to have a pretty good sense of the absurd. That's why having a Wicked Good Sense of Humor is mandatory.

(Excerpt from *Yank East* Magazine's *Guide to Tourist Traps in Maine,* 1986 Edition)

RIMSHOT CAVERNS — a natural rock formation makes it possible to hear a drummer giving a "rimshot" whenever you tell a joke, even if the joke isn't funny. Comics young and old, both professionals and green amateurs, have tried their hand here. For those who aren't clever enough to come up with their own jokes, a *Guide Book of 100 of the World's Best One-Liners* is provided. Wednesday is Truly Tasteless Night, and Sunday mornings are reserved for clergy and golfing jokes...

Tell Your Own Maine Joke

Want to be the life of the party, but can't afford an accordion? Learn how to tell Maine jokes! It's easy, it's fun, and you can even make a little money doing it! Just choose an "opening line" from Column A; add a "setup" from Column B; and watch 'em roll in the aisles when you deliver the "punch line" from Column C. Caution: be sure to tell the joke in a Maine accent or nobody will get it. Remember, the humor is *very* dry!

A	B	C
Virgil Bliss was the dirtiest man in Hancock County.	She had to go in the door sideways so she wouldn't break the door jamb.	"She's up on the roof, and she won't come down."
I was sittin' on the porch of Aunt Bertha's house when one of them foreign cars came roarin' up the road.	So I went up to the lighthouse at the point and knocked on the door.	"Don't you move a God damn inch."
Every year, the ladies of the Methodist Church have a picnic out at the seashore.	That summer it was so dry that even the birds were singing with scratchy throats.	"I guess prob'ly you'd better come back Wednesday."
My Uncle Perley was as bald as an egg.	Grandfather would take him out on the lobster boat every morning at the crack of dawn.	"It ain't my dog, mister."
Arthur Dingley was married quite late in life.	After the cat drowned in the well, we all thought it was going to be a hard winter.	"Of course your horse is blind. I told you when I sold it to you that it don't look so good."

Tarmac The Magnificent

ED: We have with us in the studio a visitor from the East. From the far Down East, in fact. He has the ability to look through concrete, at least that's what he told the girls' gym coach in high school. Ladies and gentlemen, welcome please, Tarmac the Magnificent!

BAND: (Plays something appropriately Oriental as Tarmac arrives wearing a red-and-black-checked hat, a tattered bathrobe and a towel under the hat. He trips just before he arrives at the interview table.)

ED: Greetings oh wise and great one.

TARMAC: Hello to you, kerosene breath.

ED: I have an empty mayonnaise jar containing several sealed envelopes. In these envelopes are questions which have been written by a sixth-grade class in Palmyra, Maine. No one, not even the Maine State Police, knows the contents of these envelopes. But you, with your ability to see through translucent glass, will be able to determine the contents of these envelopes.

TARMAC: Let's cut the jabberin' and get on with it.

ED: I have in my hand the first envelope.

TARMAC (holds envelope to head): Dolly Parton.

ED: Dolly Parton?

TARMAC: Dolly Parton. (Opens envelope, blows into it.) What do you see Dolly doin' at the barbershop after she's through cuttin'?

AUDIENCE: (Groans.)

TARMAC: Tarmac is like woodstove on January night. Rather slow getting started.

ED: I have the next envelope.

TARMAC (holds to head): A place to park and Anita Bryant.

ED: A place to park ...

TARMAC: ... and Anita Bryant. (Opens envelope.) Name two things you are unlikely to find this summer in Ogunquit ...

ED (guffaws): I have the next envelope.

TARMAC (holds envelope to head): Sap buckets.

ED: Sap buckets?

TARMAC: That's what I said. Sap buckets. (Opens envelope.) What do you find on the telephone poles in Lewiston in the springtime?

AUDIENCE: (Subdued laughter.)

TARMAC: Tarmac better renew subscription to *Reader's Digest*.

ED: I have the next envelope, Tarmac.

TARMAC: Squished budworms, dead moose, and large Christmas trees.

ED: Squished budworms...

TARMAC: ...dead moose, and large Christmas trees. (Opens envelope.) Name three things out-of-staters have on their cars as they leave the Maine woods.

ED: I have in my hand the final envelope.

AUDIENCE: (Applauds loudly.)

TARMAC: May a caravan of Winnebagos relieve itself on your front yard!

ED: (Guffaws.)

TARMAC (holds envelope to head): The Yankees, Red Sox, and the Indians.

ED: The Yankees, Red Sox, and the Indians?

TARMAC (TO ED): You do pretty good for someone whose three hardest years were fourth grade. (Opens envelope.) Who used to own the North Woods, what did they wear in the winter, and who owns the woods now?

BAND: (Plays revolting Oriental music as Tarmac bows and makes rapid exit before bottles and tomatoes are thrown on stage.)

WICKED GOOD HUMOR—AN OPPOSING VIEWPOINT

IT'S NOT FUNNY!

A Distinguished Clergyman Concludes that So-called "Real Maine" Humor Is a Menace to Society.

by the Rev. Wilhelm "Billy" Crankcase
Pastor, Corsica Church of the Dour Redeemer

The Rev. Crankcase's private chapel

"Wicked Good" — The name conjures up images of a Maine ruled by a benign idiocracy living in mobile homes, decorating their lawns with silly ornaments, riding snowmobiles, and displaying at every turn an utter lack of even the fundamental elements of good taste. Of course, the so-called Wicked Good Mainer may also be an urbanite who always appears as a vacuous, trendy consumer, incapable of an original or authentic thought, someone who moved to Maine five years ago and thinks buying a four-wheel-drive car marks his final passage into true Mainehood.

Rural or urban, you're either one kind of jerk or another. That seems to be the message of the purveyors of the "real Maine" mystique. This creates an image of Maine no Mainer could love. It induces a Mainer's self-loathing, sending him off on a bewildering quest for a better self-image. And that makes him prime pickings for the Wicked Good Band, which has positioned itself to be Maine's new tastemaker and opinion leader.

What's wrong with all of this? First of all, the band uses gross-outs, body-parts humor, and dirty jokes to make their point. No one I know believes these are either necessary or funny!

More importantly, however, the band, with their "real Maine" humor, displays a contempt for the taste, judgment and intelligence of their fellow human beings. And therein lies the clue to their real purpose in this life.

For twenty centuries, a low opinion of humans has been the *sole province* of the various churches, true or otherwise. The idea that people are walking swamp scum, almost beyond hope, is what made religion great and keeps it strong. If Steve Bither and associates are purveying a similar notion, then by definition they have visions of themselves as religious leaders. There's simply no other explanation. *The Wicked Good Band's ultimate goal is the conversion of the state of Maine into a religious and political cult which will attempt to subvert the Nation!*

Let's consider the name, Wicked Good, a traditional Maine idiom. The phrase is a contradiction: "Wicked" and "good" cannot coexist in a single entity. And since "wicked" comes before "good" the band's very name turns out to be a symbol for its goals — the triumph of evil over good, the creation of a state where, to paraphrase Orwell, *wicked is good, good is wicked.*

The band practices the modern folly of *"secular humorism."* This is the theory that the normal foibles of Everyman and, indeed, everyday life itself can be funny.

This is, of course, false prophecy.

Anyone whose eyes have been turned by the Lord to the true path of enlightenment, as embodied in the practices of the Corsica Church of the Dour Redeemer, knows that there's nothing funny about everyday life. Life is a pesthole, an endurance test, a crucible of misery, and man is not a comedian, he is an insect doomed to endless proofs of his worthlessness to bask in the sunshine of an elusive Reward. It's just not funny! Man is not funny! And, with two exceptions, life is not funny! The two exceptions are when a labor union's employees go on strike, and AIDS.

But the Wicked Good Band, on the other hand, finds humor everywhere. And it uses this humor to teach Maine people self-loathing ... again, the sole property of organized religion.

What can we do about this menace?

The answer is simple.

Kill them!

Yes, I know that violates God's holy laws as well as the laws of man. But even a faithful moral absolutist must sometimes read between the lines. I have it on the Highest Authority that, if you kill a member of the Wicked Good Band, God will be looking the other way!

4. GROSS STATE PRODUCT

Excerpts from *What Color Is Your Trailer? — Career Goals in Maine:*

Introduction: Of all the activities that Maine people get involved with, the one activity we pursue the most eagerly, the most frequently, and least successfully, is: How to Make Money. It's only the chosen few who are fortunate enough to clean up on things like Wicked Good records and books. The rest have to go out and get a job. It isn't really difficult to get a job in Maine if you follow the guidelines put forward in *What Color is Your Trailer?*, the Maine version of the best-selling book *What Color is Your Parachute?* The approach in *Parachute* is to play up your strengths, organize yourself, and create a position that you and only you can walk into. That approach may work on a soap opera, but here in the real world things are a bit tougher...

One problem potential job seekers have is that they are too well-educated. Maine employers don't want smart people. If they need brains, they can buy a computer. They don't want people who know how much the minimum wage is supposed to be, or who know what "OSHA" means. If you want a job, say things like: "I love feeding French fries to the seagulls." Also, ask for help in spelling your name on the application.

Experience could also work against you. If you've ever had a job before in Maine, employers won't hire you. They'll think either that you're incompetent and have been fired a lot, or that you're a malcontent who quits every job you start. Instead, tell your employer that your parents supported you and you worked under the table. Depending upon what type of job you're seeking, and upon the sexual orientation of your employer, your potential boss may also ask you to work under the table.

Finally, your appearance will be crucial to your chances of obtaining employment. Don't wear your favorite buffalo-plaid hunting shirt to the interview. The boss might think you're going to want to take time off during the hunting season. Don't wear L.L. Bean clothes to the interview. The boss will think you might quit any day to return to Massachusetts.

What kinds of careers are open to you? In the old days, it used to be that you could go to work in the woods, on a boat, or in the mill. Now, things have changed and opportunities are limitless. The Canadians have all the woods jobs, out-of-staters have all the lobster licenses, and the mill just changed hands in a merger and has folded up. So you are going to have to do what everyone else does in Maine — make little ceramic busts of Elvis or paintings of kids with big eyes on black velvet. Or make antiques and sell them at yard sales. As a final resort for the totally unemployable, bone up on your Maine accent and start a career as a Maine humorist.

Discover the Mall-O-Maine — dozens of stores in climatically controlled, connected quonset huts for your shopping needs.

Shop here —

MALL-O-MAINE

Peavy's-R-Us — All your logging needs under one roof. From augers to chippers, chains to chipmunk bait — Peavys-R-Us has it. Come in now and get 25% off on all four-wheel-drive conversion kits for '67 Mercury Comets as we continue to clearcut our prices for you. (Peavys-R-Us is a division of Slash-N-Burn, Inc.)

Sperms-N-Such — One stop shopping for all your artificial insemination needs. From the economical generic sperm to the top-of-the-line celebrity, Sperms-N-Such has the little wigglers you're looking for. Shop in the Sperms-N-Such "Whoops" corner for damaged items at low, low prices. While Supplies Last!!! In honor of Elvis himselvis — prices on all Elvis-impersonator sperm have been slashed. (Look for Only Ovules, opening soon in the Mall-O-Maine.)

Kusser's Korner — Wall plaques, T-shirts, how-to books — it's Kusser's Korner for the cussing connoisseur. Free introductory courses in "The Joys of @#*!&@$@*!!!" are offered every month by the Sultan of Swear. Learn the cussing do's and don't's of smashing fingers with hammers, stubbing toes, golfing, eating piping hot chowder and much, much, more!

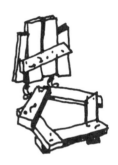

Spittoons For You — If you've been spitting for years or days, chew tobacco or have a severe respiratory disease, you'll delight at the spitting accessories available at Spittoons For You. Specializing in hocking ware for more than 25 years, Spittoons For You has the practical and the unusual. This week's specials: Lunga Guard — special wax protects the finish of your car or truck from unsightly spit marks; and Looey Lounger, a Barcalounger-type chair with dentist's spit bowl conveniently attached to the arm (plumbing not included).

Backhouse Boutique — Backhouses, backhouse accessories, and backhouse-like accessories for your indoor facilities are "in" again. On sale now: two-seater toilet. Replace that unsightly single porcelain bowl and tank with a fully-plumbed, wooden, two-seater toilet and spend more "quality time" with your family.

Your U-Joint, Sir — Discover the joys of transmitting rotation from one shaft to another at Your U-Joint, Sir. Universal joints for all cars and all occasions. If you have a shaft that is not collinear with another shaft, you need a U-joint from Your U-Joint, Sir. On sale this week, the paperback edition of *The U-Joints of Maine*.

𝓛eisure 𝓢eats — Double-knit polyester seat covers for your car and home in all sizes, colors and prints — all can be yours at Leisure Seats. Now you can decorate the interior of your home and car in the same colors you wear on your back — lima bean green, canned salmon, Bic pen blue — and have the convenience of polyester. Spill some ketchup on that couch or car seat? With Leisure Seats, you simply wipe spills away with a damp sponge.

Stretch Pant Station — A trainload of stretch pants has always just pulled into Stretch Pant Station. You can choo-choo-choose from wide variety of colors, but just one style and size: stretchy, petites, juniors, and large women all look the same when they get on board the fashion train at Stretch Pant Station.

Rust Rustique — Hobbyists and artisans worldwide have discovered the pleasure and satisfaction of creating works of art from rust. Now you can too. All it takes is a large common household appliance, our special Rustique naval jelly and your imagination. Let the experienced sales staff at Rust Rustique show you how to apply our naval jelly to your appliance for different, creative effects. Let them show you where to put the appliance on your porch or in your yard for maximum artistic expression. Say hello to the folks at Rust Rustique and discover the lucrative world of art.

And when you want a break from shopping, have a snack at one of these fine establishments in our "Gourmet Quonset" food mall:

Slice-O-Beets — Succulent slices of beets — deep-fat fried to a golden purple — and stuffed beet peels.

Make Mine Tripe — Tripe, the way you like it! Tripe on a bun, tripe on a stick. Tripe, tripe, tripe!

Cuppa Beans — Maine-made beans in a paper cup. Redeye, kidney, soldier and pea, all smothered in our special ketchup sauce.

Mousse of Maine — All Maine mousse. Blueberry mousse, lobster mousse, potato mousse, moose mousse. Mousse, mousse, mousse!

I-HOO (International House of Oatmeal) — Oatmeal served in more than 300 ways with an international touch.

Spamburgers Plus — That American classic canned luncheon meat, served in one-eighth-pound slabs with unmelted Velveeta cheese on white bread. You'll love it!

TACKY TRINKETS

My aunt Bessie has a gift shop down on Old Route One.
From Memorial to Labor Day it's the scene of lots of fun.
The Big Cars from New Jersey all stop at her door.
And visitors come clamoring in. Here's what they're looking for:

A picture of a lighthouse, a bright red plastic lobster.
She always charges double, no matter what it costs her.
The tourists snap them right up, they never seem to holler!
Even when she sells them four clamshells for a dollar.
She makes lots of money always, no matter shine or rain,
Selling Tacky Trinkets to the Tourists...
Exploiting the coast of Maine.

Some are fat and forty with French perfume and paint.
They like to stop at Bessie's; they say, "Isn't this quaint?"
Uncle Hiram tells a Maine joke that he heard from *Bert and I.*
Which serves as an inducement for them to buy, buy, buy!
A ceramic seagull ashtray, usually quite large,
For $16.95 plus tax, cash or Mastercharge.
On the back shelf you will find a gift to set you back a small sum —
A scented pillow with the words, "Fir you I pine, I even balsam."
She makes her yearly income, before the autumn rains,
Selling Tacky Trinkets to the Tourists...
Exploiting the coast of Maine.

From postcards to old pine cones,
She even has a lobster trap decked out in rhinestones...
Tacky Trinkets to the Tourists, exploiting the coast of Maine.

The Flea Market

If Karl Marx were to investigate the economic principles of the Maine flea-market economy, he might revise his view that capitalism will bury itself. Whatever has been buried, or should have been buried, will come to life again and again in Maine at a flea market.

Cousin Perley has had a flea market at his barn every Saturday for the past three years. The barn has never emptied much, even though a lot of things have been sold. It's sort of like the "bottomless cup of coffee" at the Miss Brunswick Diner. It just never seems to end, no matter how badly you want it to.

Perley doesn't just buy and sell flea market material. He adds an extra twist — he uses thing for a while, then he'll put them back on the market. He might buy, say, a butter dish for hi wife, have her use it for four or five months, an put it out on the table in the barn for a little mor than he originally paid for it.

There's a standing rule at Perley's house that yo don't use the same salt-and-pepper shaker fo more than a month. I was over there for dinner las Friday. "Clean up after you eat," he said. "Thes dishes are going on sale tomorrow." And of cours Perley isn't too particular what gets sold at the fle market. When Bertha Kern's boy left his sled ove to Perley's house last winter, Perley "lost" it.

Perley's favorite saying in his younger days wa

"You never can tell when it'll come in handy." This was his stock line for saving everything. He learned that line from his father, who started the massive family collection over sixty years ago with some *Youth Companions*. They added *National Geographics* (they found the issues featuring half-naked African women sold particularly well), mystery code rings purchased with Wheaties box tops, sets of china from Woolworth's, every license plate in town from 1930 onward and probably every nut, bolt, nail, or screw that they had used in the past forty years.

Mother is cynical about Perley. She sees through the "thrifty Yankee" image. "He's not thrifty. He's cheap," she says. "He never bought a new thing in his life." Mother thinks Perley's success has changed people's attitudes. "Years ago, he was considered a pack rat. Now, because he's saved everything, he's a visionary. It used to be that having that big old house and having to heat it was a liability. Now, since he's got more space to store more junk, it's a major asset."

I like to go to Perley's on Saturday for a review of the reading matter. Perley has a hidden streak of culture somewhere — either that or he traded something for several years' worth of *The New Yorker*. They fit right in with the *Life* magazines. A recent study by the Maine Department of Flea Markets determined that of all of the *Life* magazines sold in Maine between 1940 and 1960, 61.2% are still extant, and half have already been resold at flea markets. Perley figures he's easily paid back the subscription prices on every magazine he's ordered just by letting it molder a bit in the barn for twenty years until somebody buys it at a higher price than it sold for new.

Mother always goes for the figurines, despite her opinion of Perley. She got a gorgeous elf under a mushroom that was an exact miniature of the big one we got in the yard. She had to shake her head in admiration when we got to the canning jars. Perley's wife had bought these twenty years ago for thirty-five cents each, used them for twenty years to put up zucchini pickles, and now here they were for ten bucks. I'm surprised Harvard Business School hasn't called Perley down to teach a few courses.

Now here's a real treasure — an old 78 RPM recording of Rufus Dufus and the Duffers: "It's Springtime, That's Why I'm Scratching," with the cow and pig duo.

Mother looks at me with disgust: "Let's go," she says. "I can stand someone making money off other people's stupidity, but I can't stand him making money off his own dishonesty."

"What do you mean, is he creating antiques again?" I ask.

"No, it's this little milk bottle from Gushee's Dairy. He didn't return it forty years ago, and now he's getting five dollars for his thievery. And poor Gushee went out of business, probably because no one returned their milk bottles."

"Look," I tell her, "it all works out. See this brown-ribbed Orange Crush bottle that he's selling for two dollars? He found it last week under the floorboards of the barn. And all that time he never got his two cents back."

"I suppose you're right. What are we gonna do with all this stuff we got today, anyway?"

"Put it in the barn with the stuff we bought last week," I tell her. "Like the man says, you never can tell when it'll come in handy."

ARE THEY WICKED GOOD?

We asked our Panel of Experts:

IS WICKED GOOD	AIN'T
Products that use "o" instead of "of" in their brand names	American companies using Scandinavian or Dutch names on products that aren't imported
Retail businesses named "Mr..."	Retail businesses with puns in their names
Splitting malls	Maine Mall
Large billboards advertising tacky junk at gift shops	Informational kiosks
Police scanners	Scanners at the grocery store checkout counter
5% passbooks	Credit cards
Dollar bills crumpled into balls	Susan B. Anthony dollars
"Cash" transactions (i.e., under the table)	Checks with pictures on them

5. THE WICKED GOOD PAST

Legends O'the Sea

The Maine seacoast is filled with lore of yore: exciting tales of those brave men, those dastardly cowards, and those mysterious events which put Maine on the maritime map, but were otherwise forgotten. So mizzen the main foxle, don't slip on the poop deck, and gather 'round ye mateys.

VELMA'S THIGH

Ask any lobsterman who's worked the southern tip of Dingley Bay, and they'll tell you about Velma's Thigh. It's about six feet of ledge, exposed only at very low tide. Anyone who gets within a half mile of it will hear a high-pitched, nasal voice, shriller than the harpies of old. Vinal Beal swears that he hears his wife saying: "I wish to God you'd learn to put that toilet seat down! I nearly fell right in last night!" Albie Mitchell heard the voice saying: "If you don't take your boots off before you come in the house I'll cuff you one up side o' the head!" And Dougie Bogan won't even go within a mile of the place after he heard the voice saying: "Of *course* I have a headache. If you'd only

let me buy a decent pair of shoes once in a while I wouldn't have a headache all the time." The fishermen and casual sailors are thankful for these warnings, however.

THE CHOWDAH BUCKET

The Chowdah Bucket is an old, rotting hulk in Casco Bay. It lies there in the middle of the clam flats exuding a Downeast quaintness along with the low-tide odor. Many folks have made it a point to visit the old ship at least once per year on their visit to Maine. Most folks make it a point *not* to visit more than once per year, however. Those who did visit thought this would be the last year it would be around. Little did they know that people had been thinking this for the past fifty-three years.

The Chowdah Bucket was originally a three-masted schooner, the *Leona Morrison*. She was never a very pretty boat. In fact, she was sold at a boatyard "seconds" dealer in Freeport. She made four or five coastal trips, carrying spuds out to the quarrying islands and lumber to Saco. But her seaworthiness was never top-notch and she was soon set aground at low tide and left to rot.

An enterprising character, Elliot Linwood, bought the *Leona* cheap and towed her up the river a bit, letting her continue to rot in some proper mud flats.

Although the neighbors were appalled, summer visitors were charmed by its quaintness. Linwood set out a hot-dog and clam-cake stand near this photo opportunity. The next year he opened up a restaurant on the boat itself, with authentic Maine cooking, as authenticated by Mrs. Linwood.

When the original *Leona* became so rotted that even Linwood wouldn't walk around her, he had another built exactly like her, with imitation rotted wood covering a solid steel framework. The first Chowdah Bucket was so successful that Linwood started a chain of steel-framed, quaintly-rotting boats that have never been to sea.

Many restauranteurs have copied the original Linwood idea and made fortunes off the quaintness of decay. The Chowdah Bucket remains as a monument to the pioneers of Maine capitalism who exploited the Maine seacoast and kept their profits high and dry.

THE GORGES FAMILY

Maine was originally patented by the King of England to Sir Fernando Gorges. It was said that Gorges lost a card game with the King and got Maine as a consolation prize. Gorges himself never set foot in the savage land, preferring the warmth and comfort of civilized England, but his name received fame in Maine by the seafaring exploits of his son and grandson.

His son, George Gorges, tried to wrestle with the problem of Maine settlement, but he throttled every money-making effort he tried, kept his creditors on the ropes, and eventually lost his life in a duel with a distant relative of a famous naval hero who, because of his short stature, had received the sobriquet "Half Nelson."

George's son was known only as Boy. He kept in fashion long after it was out of fashion to be in fashion. Because of his outrageous style of dress he was immediately identified as being from away. Most sailors refused to work on Boy's ships, but several men from Ogunquit volunteered readily and stayed with Boy for years and years.

Boy Gorges ended the Gorges dynasty because he never found the right woman to father his children. But his maritime exploits lived on for generations. Boy discovered Old Orchard Beach when his ship went aground there loaded with trinkets for the settlers of the St. John River.

Milton M. Young's cigars in his museum

Hats Off!

To Milton M. Young
    Civil War Victim
        Writer
            Creator of Red-and-Black-Checked Caps

Milton M. Young, a name nearly forgotten today, stands in the Wicked Good Hall of Fame for his contributions to Maine living. His name and memory also live on in the Milton M. Young Museum, one of the world's smallest museums, located on a shelf in Portland. The museum contains his photo, some letters, his cigars, and the world's first red-and-black-checked cap.

Milton M. Young, a gallant Maine lad, loved to go hunting. He used to wear just a plain cotton hat during hunting season, but found the November wind extremely cold on his head. One night, seeing his mother mend a red-and-black-checked woolen shirt, he came upon the idea of placing the wool on the cap and using excess pieces of wool for ear flaps. The result was a big success and allowed Milton M. Young to hunt throughout the winter without ever getting frostbite on his ears.

Spring, 1862: The drumbeats of war reach Milton's hometown, and he is called to fight. He joins the legendary 20th Maine Regiment and peforms gallantly. His letters home, still preserved in the Milton M. Young Museum, talk of the battles and the ordinary events of life. They also reflect his fascination with hats: "Saw a corporal in the New York Grenadines today," he wrote in March, 1863. "He was wearing a four-cornered cap made of lambswool and leather bearing the company insignia. Looks wicked sharp."

It was at the Battle of Gettysburg that the 20th Maine, and Milton M. Young, saw their finest hour. He was shot by a Reb wearing a gray beaverskin hat with a long red feather in it. Milton was standing up to get a closer look when the Reb gunned him down.

Milton had found in his prewar years that when he wore the red-and-black hat out hunting in the woods he was less likely to get shot at by other hunters. He thought it brought him luck. If only he had been wearing his famous creation on that fateful day in Gettysburg, the world might have heard more from him. He could have even surpassed Farmington's Chester Greenwood, inventor of the earmuffs. We will never know. Instead we offer a tip of the hat to the memory of Milton M. Young.

The original Milton M. Young hat

Maine's Forgotten Literary Map

From Longfellow to Stephen King, from Artemus Ward and Kate Douglas Wiggin to Kenneth Roberts and May Sarton, Maine has produced more than its share of literary giants. But for every superstar, there are scores of lesser figures, writers whose life work has been undervalued or forgotten, sometimes with good reason. Tourists making the rounds of famous writers' homes may want to add these landmarks to their itineraries.

BERWICK — For six decades, the graceful light verse of Thelma Barks Verrill (1849-1938) charmed subscribers of the *Saturday Evening Post* and a host of smaller publications. With gentle wit and country common sense, she described the foibles of everyday life in rural Maine with a universal touch that made her beloved as a popular voice of small-town America. "Wash the car and watch it rain; / Leave the crud and scorch the grain," she wrote in 1908, uttering what has become one of the nation's favorite middle-class cliches. Forgotten for more than forty years, she has been restored to her rightful place in American letters by the recently published Harvard University Press eight-volume study, *The Literary Ancestors of Erma Bombeck*. The family farm in Berwick houses a small museum, including her papers, aprons, and the famous whisk broom she so often wrote about.

CORSICA — Because his masterpiece was suppressed by censors for more than a century, Hezekiah (Volemeat) Hussey (1791?-1844?) is all but forgotten today. But Maine has never produced another literary pioneer with his stunning range. He virtually invented two of today's most popular literary genres. And yet no one in the pantheon of Maine letters is less likely to have turned to writing. Hussey was a notorious brigand, smuggler, forger, petty thief, rustler, graffiti artist, and ne'er-do-well, a familiar but unwelcome figure in the waterfront dives of a score of Kennebec River towns. His *Letter from Pownalborough Gaol* (1820) was the first published prison diary. Later he scandalized a nation with his hilarious, fraudulent account of a purported career in bestiality, *Trout Frisking in America* (1843), the first fictional sexual memoir. To this day, writing about unkind behavior to animals has remained a family custom among his descendants, who still occupy the old family shack in Corsica.

GILEAD — Today many people know Artemus Bragdon as "the Samuel Pepys of Maine." But during his lifetime (1817-1874), few people outside his home town ever heard of Bragdon. A life-long sawmill worker, Bragdon faithfully recorded the highlights of every single day of his life from the

The Verrill Homestead Museum

Hussey Family Homestead

age of nine until shortly before his death. Sadly, Bragdon never traveled, witnessed no great events, met no famed personages of his day, had little interest in the doings of his townspeople, and was not blessed with any powers of observation or interpretation. Nevertheless, his *Diaries*, published by the local historical society after his death, remain the most comprehensive daily look at nineteenth-century Maine. His succinct comments ("SUNDAY, 5 MAY, 1861: To church in the morning. A sermon on sin, and why we should be agin it. Turnip for dinner, thence to bed") provide an exhaustive if uneventful recording of a Maine rural life. Because of its unrelenting dullness, Bragdon's *Diaries* has remained a standard part of the Maine public school curriculum for nearly one hundred years.

KENNEBUNK — When the Gay '90s gave way to the Fairly Dull Single Numbers, America entered a long period of conservative social mores. Women bore the brunt of the repressive rules of the times. Young women were supposed to stay home in an extended study of homemaking skills until the right marriageable gentleman came along. Only a few voices encouraged women to get out, kick up their heels, and enjoy themselves. The most popular was Mable Holmes Parks (1873-1943). Her daringly saucy light verse in such magazines as *Monocle* and *Kat's Meow* helped set the tone for that long-ago era. Young women blushed when

Entrance to the Parks Collection Annex at the Kennebunk Library

they read couplets such as, "When Amos played a ragtime tune/I flushed, I gasped, I flip't, I swooned," but they hid the poems from their parents and read them over and over. Mild though her work may seem today, Parks' poetry scandalized Kennebunk, and she eventually left town in disgrace. Though she continued writing until her death, she never enjoyed the following and fame that were hers before the Roaring Twenties, whose spirit she helped usher in, swept her aside. The local public library has the most complete collection of her published work.

LEWISTON — What true Maine hunter of the last half-century would venture into the woods without two books, the L.L. Bean *Catalogue* and Réné Retourneau's *Guide to the Maine Woods*? Retourneau (b. 1890) began writing his popular *Lewiston Daily Sun* outdoors column, "Nimrod at Large," in 1914. His command of the lore of the forest, and his skill with rod and reel, gained him an avid following which for decades looked to him as the ultimate authority on fish and game matters. The *Guide*, published in 1939, remains the standard reference book. In 1948, all of New England followed the intense nineteen-day search when Retourneau was lost in treacherous forests surrounding Highland Lake in Falmouth. His survival of the ordeal was all the more remarkable because he had lost six toes and his left forearm in seven hunting accidents over the years. Retired since 1955, he still contributes an occasional essay to the *Sun*, which has published several collections of his columns, *A-Hunting We Will Go*, *A-Fishing We Will Go*, and *A-Trapping We Will Go*.

MASARDIS — A small museum here preserves the personal effects of Lancelot Dulac (1795-1863), author of one of America's most beloved jokes. Dulac, known locally as a wit with a dry, ironic sense of humor so typical of Maine humorists, enjoyed a friendly rivalry with Dr. Romeo Boucher for the unofficial title of Masardis' top wag. One day during the harvest, Dulac fell from a wagon. A potato broke his fall, but became wedged in his ear so firmly that all efforts to remove the spud failed. Dulac was rushed to Dr. Boucher's office. When the doctor saw his friend, he quipped, "What's wrong, Lance?" The men carrying Dulac laughed so hard they nearly dropped him. Never one to pass up a good line, Dulac retorted: "I can't hear you, Doc, I got a potato in my ear." Today that

bon mot is one of only seven American jokes to break into the charmed one-hundred-million re-tellings circle, and it was the first gag formally designated a National Historic Joke by the National Humor Preservation Commission.

WISCASSET — With his trademark beard, his patented accent, and his endless columns, books, and lectures, Cal Callitwell is Maine's most ubiquitous and most widely recognizable contemporary writer. Some people favor his lyrical descriptions of Maine's natural beauty, while others prefer the verbal tapestries he weaves as he describes the lives of the humble-but-honest fishermen, artisans, and tradespeople who comprise the noble peasantry of Callitwell's Maine. But it is as a chronicler of the elite upon which his reputation rests. Unfailingly sycophantic in the presence of the politically powerful, unwaveringly lavish in his descriptions of Maine's unfortunately-not-so-idle -rich, Callitwell has earned his niche as a voice for the American yearning for upward mobility. "Perhaps no American writing today more accurately reflects the heart and soul of the career social climber," says the *Providence Provident*.

Cal Callitwell's boat collection at their usual moorings.

Wicked Good Things That Are No Longer with Us

Before the Yuppies took over Portland's Old Port, there was M.A. Sulkowitch. You could get hardware on one side of the store and clothes on the other. Stuff like DeeCee overalls, Gorilla work boots, wool bathing suits. A member of the Wicked Good Band bought a pair of wool pinstripe double-pleated slacks there. You can still see the mark on the legs where the pants had been folded in 1936.

42

DOT'S BEAUTY TRAILER: Before the outlets took over Freeport, there was Dot's — a Beauty Salon in a Trailer. We confess to never having visited Dot's, but imagine the bouffants, the blue hair, and the wicked gossip that must have been created there.

THE CRANK THAT GOT YANKED

The little town of Bryant Pond, Maine, got national media recognition as it unsuccessfully put up a battle with the corporate Goliaths over the issue of what kind of phone system to use in the town. Townspeople had been pretty happy with a crank system, like Jeff used to use on Lassie. But when a bigger company took over the locally owned system, they replaced the crank with their own style of phones.

BRYANT POND (to the tune of "Memphis")

Long Distance Information won't you give me Bryant Pond?
I ain't been able to reach there since they put those new phones on.
I'm tryin' to reach Bill who lives over on South Street
About a half a mile from the plant where they make the concrete.

Last time I saw Bill he was gonna put a weld in my gas tank,
But I ain't been able to hear from him since they went and yanked the crank.
If you can't reach him, surely his next door neighbor Velma will.
She's that rather large woman in the blue trailer that sets up there on the hill.

Long Distance Information, God Damn that AT&T!
I'm just trying' to get in touch with Bill and I know he's tryin' to get in touch with me.
Since they took out all the phones and put the new ones up on the wall,
Bill still has his crank one left, and he can't call at all.

YANKEAST MAGAZINE

The Magazine For People Who Don't Live In Maine, But Who Have A Better Idea About What Maine Is Supposed To Be Like Than The People In Maine Do Themselves.

I Love Maine

by Cal Callitwell

Cal Callitwell's picnic table

Maine. I love Maine. Beautiful Maine, with its crisp, clear, blue ocean, its great, cool, crisp, green pines, and its hot, steamy crisp red lobsters. I love lobsters. My wife Carolyn loves lobsters, too. And I love my wife, Carolyn: tall, tan, crisp Carolyn.

Carolyn was, as always, first mate on the Bard, our catboat, on our afternoon sail through the cool, crisp, blue waters of Casco Bay. There was a clean, brisk, almost crisp wind at our backs and a myriad of islands ahead on starboard and port.

First, let me say about Maine's islands: I love these islands. So does Carolyn. They contain history, adventure, and a cool, crisp hiding place from the everyday cares of the harsh world.

Today our destination was Hog's Snout, site of an exciting part of Maine's future. In addition to being first mate on the Bard, Carolyn is a real estate broker working on developing Hog's Snout into condos. We love Maine's islands. We love Maine people. But more than any of these things, we love money...green, crisp money.

Awaiting us on the island were Cad and Buffy Perkins from Philadelphia, owners of Hog's Snout through inheritance from Buffy's uncle, Capt. Ray Quickprint. We always kid Buffy that Capt. Ray made his money running hooch during Prohibition, but Buffy will only smile with her crisp, gray eyes and say: "Uncle Ray never talked much about his past." We scoured the island looking for the captain's treasure, but only found empty bottles of Old Duke Pink, for which the Captain had developed a fondness in his later years.

For lunch, we had quiche, champagne and tan, crisp Doritos. We discussed work in progress dredging the inlet for a marina and blasting the ledge on the Snout's tip for a better depth for the big boats. Some local lobstermen had been a tad upset about this disturbance to their grounds, but Cad, who gives good credence to the term Philadelphia lawyer, settled their problems to our satisfaction.

Our repast and business over, we got back aboard the Bard and back out to the refreshing, crisp bay breezes, with the sound of the seagulls wheeling overhead mingling perfectly with the occasional explosions of the blasting crew and the crisp sound of shotgun volleys loosed by the fishermen at the blasting crew.

Ahead through the shimmering sky was the familiar skyline of our home port, as I expertly guided the Bard to her berth. My thoughts turned to having a cool, crisp gin and tonic, then sitting down at my typewriter and writing my adventures on crisp, white sheets of paper. I love writing, especially about Maine. Because, if I haven't told you before, I'll let you in on a big secret: I love Maine.

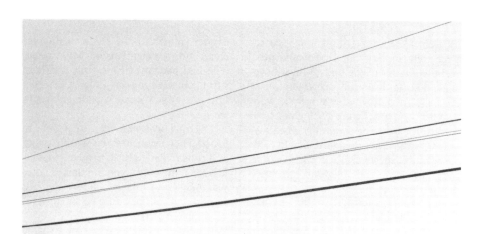

Memories of A Quaint New England Town

by Sally Cushing

I remember my little town as if it were yesterday. The quaint little streets, the little men that ran the little stores, and the great big paper mill at the end of our street. Everybody in town worked in the mill. They told us we were lucky to live that close to work. One time I told Mom it didn't smell very nice being that close to the paper mill. She got angry with me and told me it was the "sweet smell of success."

That's what the Chamber of Commerce called it, too, so I guess Mom must have been right.

I remember our quaint little New England-style house. It had been white, but somehow it was always a dingy brown. My sister and I helped Mom do the laundry, but we learned never to hang the white sheets outside, because they didn't come back in that way.

Oh, and the cute little church that we

all went to. Pastor Dillingham used to pray each Sunday that God would protect the owners of the mill. It must have shaken his faith several years later when the mill closed down after it merged with another company. Pastor Dillingham performed the wedding ceremony when my sister Christine got pregnant. She looked so beautiful in her white gown. It got a little dingy at the end of the day, but it was nice in the morning.

Every year in the middle of the summer the town would have Old Foam Days down by the riverside. We girls played "rot the pot" by putting a metal pot in the river and seeing how fast the metal would rot away. The boys played "foam toss." Our dads played softball and drank beer. And our moms sat in the shade and gossipped. The highlight of the day was the crowning of "Miss Foamy." I was runner-up one year to the mill manager's daughter.

The little businesses on Main Street met our every need. When a shopping mall came in and people noticed that prices "downstreet" were somewhat higher, many of the little businesses closed up. I remember old Mr. Franginelli and his fruit. If the fruit had been sitting outside for a day or so, it looked a little dusty and it made you kind of sick to eat it.

The mill was real nice to people in town. They published the weekly paper and contributed to the Chamber of Commerce. Whenever someone started complaining, he would be shown the bus station and told he could go to Russia if he wanted a change.

My little town changed a lot after the paper mill closed down. Finally, a new owner and a new use was found for the mill...a pesticide plant. On my little street, all the trees that used to be in front of our house are gone, as are most of the gardens and lawns. The children seem to look a little funny, but that might be because my eyesight has dimmed with age. But the Chamber of Commerce is still active, defending the new sweet smell of success and showing those who question things the way to the bus station... Some things in life never change.

Making It with Maine

Having a Tub of Fun

What product is made in Maine, sold in twenty-seven countries around the world, and represents good, clean fun everywhere it's found? Ask anyone in West Enfield and they'll tell you: tubs from Tubby Blake, a real Maine entrepreneur whose past failures haven't prevented him from a "tub" of successes. You've probably seen the tubs if you have travelled at all. They are sold in gift shops everywhere. They stand two inches high by two inches wide and six inches long. They are in the shape of a bathtub, and they have the words "Having a Tub of Fun in Altoona, Pa." or wherever the gift shop is located. These fine-looking pine novelties are made right here in Maine at the Blakes' "tubworks." Tubby Blake's barn stands as a monument to free enterprise.

In the early 1950s when Blake moved to West Enfield from Cleveland, he had planned to take up chinchilla ranching. "I had a couple of hundred critters running around in here," he told our *Yank East* reporter on a tour of the barn last spring. "I had them for four years, but I only made money one year." He pointed to a Stetson hat on the wall and a little piece of rope in the shape of a lariat. "That's all that's left of the operation. Those chinchillas ate through everything I had. I had to learn woodworking to keep the ranch in shape, building all those little corral fences and such." After closing down the chinchilla ranch, Blake tried the lawn-ornament business. He did fairly well with the ducks, but ran into trouble with lawn jockeys. "All of a sudden, colored people weren't in style. And all the jockeys was black. Aunt Jemima and Amos 'n' Andy were out," he complained, "and I was stuck with about one hundred fifty lawn jockeys." Making the best out of a bad situation, he was able to sell his remaining jockeys at half price after he had painted them white. He sold a few unpainted ones at full price to some nostalgic John Birchers in New Hampshire. With the money he made from the jockey clearance, he remodeled his house, adding indoor plumbing.

As the old claw-foot tub sat in the dooryard, neighbor Arthur Dingley, who possessed every joke from *Reader's Digest* and the Bennett Cerf joke books, remarked: "Looks like you're going to have a tub of fun this summer." This got Blake to thinking. "I took a couple of lathes from the old outhouse we were tearing down. I sawed and hammered at 'em. Arthur did the painting. We brought a dozen wooden tubs to the church fair that September." The first tubs were of varying size and made with different types of wood. The clever saying, "Having a Tub of Fun at the Methodist Ladies Auxiliary Fair," was a big hit and all the tubs were snapped right up. The novelty concept first spread to other New England states. His "Having a Tub of Fun in Effingham Falls, NH" is on display at the New Hampshire Trinket Museum. It wasn't long before the rest of the country was sending in orders, as well as the Carribean Islands tourist shops. When he broke into the European market, he had to hire translators to write the slogans. He did a brisk market, though, in English-only tubs. "Having a Tub of Fun in Monte Carlo" stands proudly on Blake's desk. He has heard from several collectors, including a woman in Iowa who has tubs from one hundred forty-nine locations.

Blake generally uses Maine pine in his tub creations, although lately he has been tempted to use spruce to save money. His operation employs thirty people year-round and makes for him, well, a "tub of money." But Tubby Blake doesn't intend to just sit there soaking it in. He has worked with Arthur Dingley in the development of a new product using pine cones. A source at the Tubworks, who asked to remain anonymous, but whose name is Ralph Perkins, told us that Tubby has gotten onto the health kick and that he'll be marketing small, fresh pine cones as Nature's Suppository sometime in the near future.

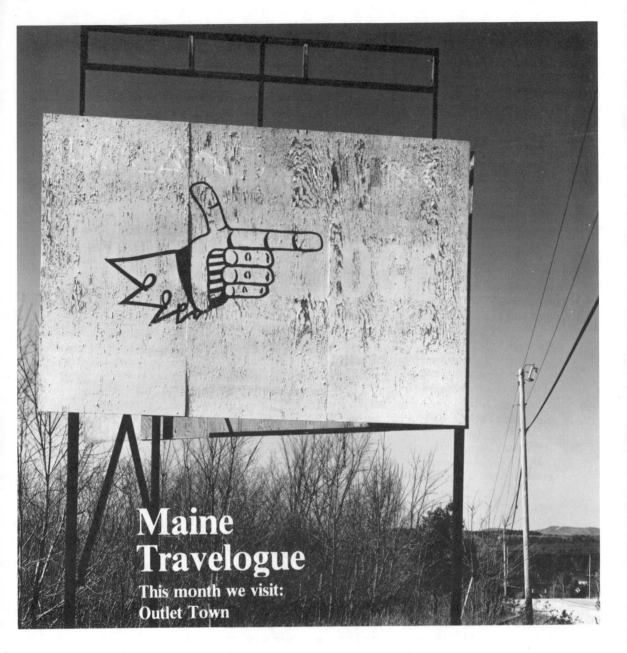

Maine Travelogue

This month we visit: Outlet Town

Mainers love bargains. That's why Maine folks and folks from away have been flocking to Outlet Town. We took the entire *Yank East* staff on a bus journey to this charming town.

The road was bumpy on the way down, even though we had heard it was a new road. We found out later that factory-second paving materials had been used and the contractor was someone who had charged a lot less. The bus was rather old, too — it used to be a school bus.

We started our day at the Breakfast Outlet, where our factory-second orders consisted of half-dried eggs and luke-warm coffee. Then it was off to the shops and the bargains. Julie bought a pair of pants with only one leg. Barb found a gorgeous sweater with no neck hole. They didn't really care if the quality was off — they had gotten a *bargain!*

Then it was off to a series of manu-facturer's outlets. These were being visited by lots of out-of-state visitors who had quite a lot of money. The "bargains" offered in these stores were listed as being forty percent. Unfortunately this was forty percent off things that were already two hundred percent what they should cost. But around the corner at a little abandoned gas station we found some of the best bargains of the day. New — or almost new —stereo equipment, clothing and jewelry at incredible prices! No one in our group cared where the stuff came from, because they had found another *bargain!*

Lunch time in Outlet Town can be a bit disconcerting for the first-time visitor. We ate at a factory-second fast-food place where the service was quite slow. We spent the rest of our afternoon at the specialty shops. At the Outlet Outlet we got some good prices on our electrical needs. At the Inlet Outlet we were able to buy a few pieces of coastal property. (Jeanette found later, however, that the piece of tidal river frontage she had purchased was really a heap of clam shells that could only be reached at low tide.) Finally, it was time for the visit to the State O'Maine Outlet, where there were selected portions of Piscataquis County

at incredible bargain rates, but nobody was buying.

We made our weary way back to the tour bus for the trip home. But there was no bus —our driver had sold this, too. We at first got mad, but then realized that this was a way of life in Outlet Town. We should be happy for the people who bought the bus because they had really gotten a *bargain.*

Inns, Resorts & Restaurants
of Maine

Places we know you will like ...

P&M's GOURMET DINER: Where can you find duck à l'orange, with home fries and a bottomless cup of coffee? At P&M's Gourmet Diner, Route 16, Brunchville. You'll also enjoy the fried tripe and paté, the hot turkey sandwich with gravy and truffles, and the Breakfast Delight — three eggs any style, steak tartare, and blueberry juice. On the jukebox, listen to Tammy Wynette doing selections from *Aïda* and Luciano Pavarotti doing "Mama Hated Diesels So Bad."

JOHNSON ISLAND — Route 12, Johnsonville. The manager of Johnson Island, Gus Johnson, points out the charm in

Sign at P&M's Gourmet Diner

two important words: "No surprises." The food, served by Evan Johnson, is always the same. The cabins are kept homey by Bertha Johnson. You can pay extra for your gas and get wrong directions from "Bud" Johnson's Gulf. Buy a seagull ashtray at Nettie Johnson's Gift Store. Hear a sermon at the Baptist Church by Rev. Billy Johnson or at the Unitarian Church by Rev. Chuck Johnson. Special ferry rate: Half price if your name is Johnson.

LE PET O'MAINE, Brownville Junction. All beans, all the time. And lots of beans, too. This place will give you gas when the Shell station is closed. Entertainment nightly. No smoking.

OARS-N-S'MORES HOUSE — Row, row, row to your heart's content in the rustic surroundings of this restored Girl Scout camp. Unique rowboat motif throughout, free rowboat privileges for all guests on Laughing Bunny Pond, and complimentary rowing machines in every room draw enthusiasts from all over the nation. Traditional s'mores and milk served in the Bill Dunlop Lounge every evening. Oars-N-S'mores House, Laughing Bunny Pond.

TACKYNOOK LODGE — The whole family will enjoy the nonstop sun-up-to-sun-down activities at this restored Fiat dealership on U.S. Old Route 1. The children will have a ball learning how to fingerpaint on black velvet while you are off on an educational guided tour of the architecture of Old Orchard Beach. Free Magic Fingers and Porno-Max cable TV in every room. Championship eighteen-hole miniature golf course complimentary to all guests. Learn to limbo in the Key Largo North Room to the tropical tunings of Raoul Duffé and Les Duffettes. Tackynook Lodge, U.S. Old Route 1, Knick-Knack-On-Saco.

EGGAMUFFIN INN — In the heart of poultry country, this restored henhouse is a haven for breakfast enthusiasts. The lights are on twenty-four hours a day in the Way-To-Lay Room restaurant, where you can have eggs served your favorite way and wash them down with our renowned "broiler-maker." Waiters dressed in chicken suits may break into song at any moment, as the world-famous "Keep Your Cape On Revue" appears year 'round. Dance to the many musical moods of Rhonda Lett and the Ammonia Cloud. Single, two-person, and flock rates available. Eggamuffin Inn, Cockscomb.

Eggamuffin Inn

THE NEWT AND DRAGONFLY —
Traditional Irish hospitality can always
be found in this restored root cellar deep
in the heart of Maine potato country.
Imagine feasting from the famous potato
bar in the Peel-Your-Meal Restaurant.
Dessert? Of course, have a wedge of Irish
Black Potato Cake. Then slip between
your burlap sheets and fall asleep to the
bucolic drip, drip, drip of complimentary
ground water in every room. The Newt
and Dragonfly, c/o Newt O'Walleye,
Plantation #121.

LAND-O-LOBSTAH VILLA — This is
Maine the way Mainers know it. From
the time you "pahk yah cah" in the Land-
O-Lobstah "pahkin grahj" to the time you
try to "get theyah from heeyah," you'll be
living in a world that few outsiders ever
get to see. Landmark, historic-like lighthouse replicas will light your way at night
from the main "fahmhouse" to your own
individual "bahn." But watch out! Don't
step in that cow "manoowah" on the way.
But don't worry if you do. It's a perfectly
harmless, odorless, manure-type fiber.
Sleep on your lobster-shaped, saltwater-
bed. Say "ayuh" right back to your
personal, authentic "hayseed" valet. And,
of course, eat lobster, lobster, and more
lobster in the Land-O-Lobstah Restaurant. Dance nightly to the authentically quaint strains of Rufus Dufus and
the Duffers in Ye Olde Backhouse
Lounge. Ayuh! You'll have the finest
kind-o-time at the Land-O-Lobstah.
Write Land-O-Lobstah Villa, 2 Which
Way, East Vassalboro.

The Old Salt
Reminiscences around the Old Cracker Barrel

Throw another log on the fire, willya?
What do you mean you just did? Oh,
never mind, I suppose it's warm enough
anyway. I recall sitting in this very chair
when I was a boy and whittlin'. I would
whistle as I whittled. Nowadays, I can't
whistle — blows my bridgework clean
across the room when I try. Can't whittle
neither. They took away all sharp objects
from me just before Christmas. But I do
remember this chair. Or was it the other
chair that they took to the Salvation
Army last year, the one they couldn't sell
at the yard sale? But I do remember
standing right here. Of course the stove
was in a different place at the time. It
reminds me of last summer when a feller
stopped me on the road and asked directions to Nobleboro. He kinda sat there
and waited for me to say something
clever. And I was going to say something
clever too. Except by the time I started to
say it, I couldn't remember if I had said it
or not. So I gave the feller a road map.
Why does that remind me of standing by
the stove, you ask? What difference does
it make? I had an old dog that was feeling
poorly the other day. What, did I shoot it?
No, I guess it got better. My wife was
feeling poorly the other day, though. This
old town has seen a lot of changes. I can't
remember what they are, but I know it's
different from when I was a boy, standing
here singing and whittlin'. Let me show
you pictures of my grandchildren instead.
What? You have to be going? Well, I
guess I'd better be going too. What? I am
home already? Can you imagine that.
Say, before we leave, will you put another
log on the fire?

---

*EDITOR'S NOTE: This is the last column
by the Old Salt. He was taken out back
and shot by his dog after this was written.
Be watching next month for the "New
Old Salt."*

Classified

PERSONALS

I SEEK FEMALE seal for friendship, romance, wiggling on beach, etc. Must be virgin. Box "A," Rockport.

JOIN O.A. — Out-of-Staters Anonymous. Meets at Cape Elizabeth Racquet Center Wednesdays. Learn to love Maine. Speaker: Emilio Piglani will show slides and lecture on Out-of-State Place Names in Maine.

BOOKS

CAL CALLITWELL'S great books: *Maine, I Love; Maine, Lovely Maine; My Heart Is in Maine; Love, Maine, I.* $29.95 each. Also available, almost out-of-print: Callitwell's earlier work: *I Love New Jersey.* Callitwell Bookshop, Fifth Ave., N.Y., N.Y.

TURNIPS ARE DEE-LISHOUS. 131 great recipes. $9.95, Box 17, Turnip Cove.

ANIMALS

SLUGS make great pets! Adopt one today. Details, $2.95, Slug Farm, Box X, Gardiner.

SHEEP FOR RENT. Great party fun. Box O, Ogunquit.

MUSIC

NOSEFLUTE LESSONS — Impress friends, make money. Lighter than accordion. Box N, Westbrook.

MONEY-MAKING IDEAS

MAKE BIG MONEY IN SPARE TIME. Stuff shrimp at home. Send SASE for details. Vernal Ent., Box A, Corsica.

ATTENTION MAINE REAL-ESTATE BROKERS. You can make big bucks. Move to the Southwest. Details, $2.00, Box MM, Kittery.

YOUR CAT'S FUR could be worth $$$$! Send pelt for FREE inspection. RR#3, Teaneck, N.J.

FOR SALE

TURN CANADIAN $ into Real Money. Details $1 (U.S.), Box $, Belfast.

DEC 16-21 AT PERRY'S NUT HOUSE: John Hinckley, Mon: Richard Speck. Thurs: Son of Sam. Fri. Reservations required for Sat. appearance of Gen. Haig.

30' NITE GHOST, fastest ocean-going outboard made, outfitted with spacious secret cargo hold, $150,000 or best offer. Leave bid, phone # in hollow tree near town landing, Port Clyde.

BUMPER STICKERS: "This Car Climbed Mt. Katahdin," "Ayuh, I'm from Away." "I'd Rather Be Drinking At Home." 100's of laffs. Bumperyux, Lagrange.

SCHOOLS

CN U RD DIS-U? Then you don't need a course at Biddeford School of Speed Writing. Send SASE for DTLS. Box U, Saco.

BOWDOINHAM COLLEGE — Summer courses in Beer Drinking and RV Repair. Box 000, Bowdoinham.

REAL ESTATE

HISTORIC AUGUSTA HOME for rent. Occupant must also be for sale. Comes with tennis court, pool table. Easy walk to office. 4-year tenants only. Previous residents need not apply. Me. State Government, Augusta.

SMELT SHACK CONDOS: Tired of having to wait for a rental during your favorite time of the year? We've got lots and lots of condos at the right price. Box SSC, Bowdoinham.

THIS PLACE FOR SALE. Contact Generic Properties, The Road, The County.

CAMP FUNNY UNCLE

Calling ALL BOYS!

for big boys, small boys, farm boys, city boys, tom boys and mom's boys.
WE LIKE BOYS
And Boys Like Our Camp...
Brie Pond, Athens, Me.

Learn Business the Maine Way
at

CAMP SA-CHA-DEEL

Learn Antique Making, Lobster Pot Manufacture, Price Structuring by License Plate. Make Bucks Young! Route One, Commerce, Me.

ESSAABAGO ECAMPI

The Nation's only ALL ESPERANTO CAMPING EXPERIENCE! You'll be a pro at such useful terms as: "Sit down in the canoe before you tip the damn thing over!" and "I would like a plate of eels, please." Box 2121, Laca Lingua, Me.

CAMP BIRDS 'N BEES

Learn sex the fun way with total strangers that you'll never see again.

Everything included: scripts, cigarettes, showers.

Box 6996, Paris, Me.

Pierre Katahdin™
DESIGNER JEANS

The jeans designed with the Maine person in mind. The jeans that you can wear:

- When you're working on your skidder;
- When you're bowling—even with the big balls;
- When you're driving your skidder to the bowling alley.

The jeans that are made to be worn for years at a time, so that they litterally become part of you.

Some of the features:

Black Fly

Perma-Stain Fabric (every little stain will last as long as the jeans do)

And our patented, rich, full bottom, designed so that when you are bending over to change the chains on your skidder, or to hoist up a lobster trap, your family and friends will be reminded of our favorite mountain, Mt. Katahdin.

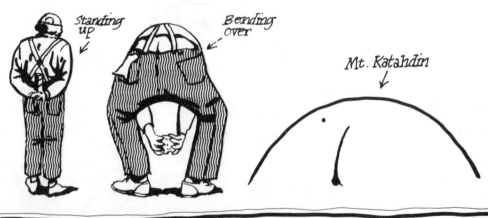

Standing up

Bending over

Mt. Katahdin

7. WICKED GOOD FASHION

A salute to that giant of the Maine fashion scene, Pierre Katahdin, creator of Katahdin™ jeans, the jeans for the Maine lifestyle.

The Story of Pierre Katahdin

Pierre Katahdin was born Peter Schmeter on a raw March morning in 1943 in the two-bed hospital (it is now the Western Maine Medical Center) of the town of East Couture. His father, Ivan, and his mother, Catherine, brought Peter, their sixth child (there were to be five more) home to their dried-flower farm in the Couture Highlands.

There in the Highlands Peter spent an uneventful childhood, giving no inkling to his parents, neighbors or teachers of the creative genius within. After an undistinguished high school career, he enlisted in the army and was assigned to the 4th Tailor Corps, Fort Bruce, Georgia. His first major assignment was to design scarves for the Army Jazz Band.

He returned to Maine after his discharge and found a job as a cutter's assistant at Maine Hunter Fashions in Jackman. He learned his trade well, matching the checks on the red-and-black plaid as well as most of the longtime employees could. Within five years he was promoted to cutter's apprentice. Luckily, he was directed to apprentice with Paul "Lucky" Poisson, the recognized granddaddy of Maine fabric cutters. Poisson left a lasting impression on Katahdin and became a friend and patron.

With Poisson's financial help and encouragement, Pierre, as he now began to call himself, broke the creative chains of Maine Hunter designs. He opened a small boutique in Rumford, special-izing in installing grommets in denim vests.

When the grommet "look" became passé, Pierre drifted from woolen mill to army surplus store, searching for the happiness and creative freedom that eluded him. The low point came when he was forced to take a job as a handkerchief tester at the Honkerquoset Linen Mill in Sanford.

Discouraged, disillusioned, and seriously chapped at the nose, Pierre quit his job in the mill and returned to his home in the Couture Highlands. A letter to Lucky Poisson reflects his depression: "I'm searching, searching, searching. What will make me happy, Lucky? It seems so close to me sometimes. I walk through the woods and dried-flower fields surrounding my home, swatting the black flies, and there seems to be this voice speaking to me of a bright future. But what is it, Lucky? Where am I going? Who am I? Do you know me?"

Poisson, sensing the sadness of his young friend, took time off from his job and visited him in the Couture Highlands. In a postcard written to the boys back at the mill, Poisson rhapsodized about this time in the Highlands: "I am as a child again. Petie and I spend the day drinking beer and talking about fabric. Petie knows fabrics instinctively. It is a religion to him. As a lark, Petie and I have bought an old Pontiac. Petie is putting on new seatcovers and I am showing him how to cut off the trunk and put on a flatbed. I think we shall go camping. Please pick up my paycheck Friday and put it in the

Credit Union."

The two friends went camping during the last few days of Poisson's visit. First, they spent time at the Desert of Maine Campground in Freeport. Poisson noticed his friend spending more and more time wandering in the desert, muttering to himself and making cryptic sketches.

Upon leaving the Desert of Maine, the two headed north. Destination: Mount Katahdin.

Pierre spent much time on the mountain sketching. The sweeping vistas seemed to inspire in him the scope of creativity that had been eluding him for so many years. Poisson too, was happy, working on their beloved Pontiac, installing a four-wheel-drive conversion kit he had picked up at a flea market in Freeport.

On the next-to-last day of the trip, Pierre strayed too far away from camp and was unable to make it back by night. Certain that Lucky would be okay without him, he spent the night on the mountain, swatting black flies and reflecting on how to make the fashion statement he was searching for.

But when he returned to camp the next morning, he found Lucky dead beneath the beloved Pontiac!

"It was those damned designer jeans he wore," Katahdin would say. "They weren't designed for someone with a full figure to be crawling around underneath a car."

An autopsy showed that Poisson died because blood circulation had been completely cut off. "He died," Katahdin said after the funeral, "because he didn't have on a pair of jeans made for a Maine person."

The rest, of course, is common knowledge. This tragedy became a source of inspiration. Katahdin (the name he now took) dedicated his life to creating jeans for Maine people. "If I can save just one life, then my life will not be in vain," he says.

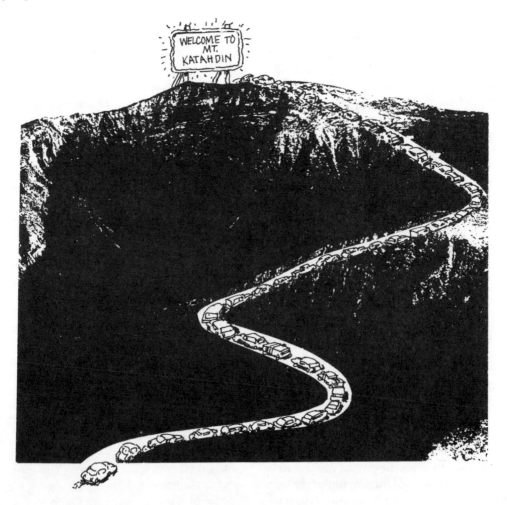

Fashions For Your Maine Lifestyle
THE POCKET TEE
Fashion Tips by Dot Tarbox
Fashion Consultant, Pierre Katahdin Jeans

When spring rolls around, the question I hear most often is: "I need some advice on tops to wear with my Katahdin™ jeans. What is the real Maine guy wearing this year?"

Summer gives us a fashion flexibility that isn't possible the other ten-and-a-half months of the year. From pool party to grease pit, there's a freedom that's ours to enjoy for those six wonderful weeks we call summer. You'll look great in almost anything you'll wear with your Katahdin™ jeans. But the proven winner year after year with that pragmatic Maine guy is the pocket t-shirt.

WHY THE POCKET TEE? The Maine guy is, above all else, practical. A well-made pocket tee, like the Pierre Katahdin™ pocket tee, will last for several years. It's easy on a Maine budget. And its heavy cotton construction absorbs perspiration, keeping the wearer comfy cool all day long. The cotton acts like a wick, trapping that perspiration with its special holding action, so that anyone can see at a glance that you work as hard in the summer as you do all the rest of the year.

Pocket t-shirts come in a small variety of drab solid colors. Any of them will go well with your new jeans. They make a quiet statement that you're too darn busy to worry about coordinating bright, flashy colors, and, like a real Maine guy, you don't want to be able to be spotted three blocks away.

The pocket tee may be a simple, even humble, garment, but like anything you wear, it has its own special language of care. If you want it to look just right, follow these simple hints:

WHEN TO BUY IT. Pick your pocket tee at the end of summer, just about the time it's becoming too chilly to wear. Why? Because you'll need all winter to break it in so that it has that genuine Maine look. Besides, over the winter you may gain or lose so much weight that the shirt won't fit right by summer, and that's what you want! A too-tight or too-baggy look on a broken-in pocket tee is a Maine fashion touch you just can't buy or fake.

HOW TO BREAK IT IN. First, you must season the shirt. In an old washtub soak the pocket tee in a mixture of detergent and Spic 'n Span. After three

Too new and stiff.

Getting better.

Ahh—just right!

weeks in the washtub, rinse in cool water. Wring the shirt vigorously, then throw it, still twisted from wringing, in a cool, dark place. Your cellar will probably be just right. Leave it alone for a month. Then all you have to do is hang it up to dry and air out, and — *voila!* It's ready to wear. *Never iron a pocket t-shirt.* That'll peg you as someone whose first driver's license didn't have a moose on the state seal.

WASHING INSTRUCTIONS: Wash your pocket tee as rarely as possible. There are no hard and fast rules on this, so let the limits of tolerance of those around you serve as a guideline for frequency of cleaning. Washing is the enemy of a fashionable pocket tee because it tends to snap the shirt back into its original shape. You want a shirt that adapts to the contours of your body, and Old Mr. Suds is your enemy.

DOT'S SPECIAL TIP. When you take off your new shirt, always pull it off by the neck. Grasp the shirt firmly at the Adam's apple, pulling the neckline straight out as far as it will go. Then, with a firm, steady motion, yank it up over your head. This will give the shirt that stretched-out neck that is essential to the look of the real Maine guy!

THE WICKED GOOD BAND

QUESTIONS FROM DOT'S MAILBOX   by Dot Tarbox,
Fashion Consultant, Pierre Katahdin Jeans

Q: *When should I wear designer logos?*

A: We at Pierre Katahdin don't think you should buy clothes that turn you into a walking billboard for fashion designers and manufacturers. But there are times when it's okay to wear something with a name on it. Some basic rules:

1. ON BASEBALL CAPS: A company or organization logo is acceptable as long as it's a Maine company and the wearer is an employee. Names of heavy-duty pickups and large trucks are allowed, but most out-of-state-firm names are discouraged. Feed and grain suppliers are okay, as long as the wearer is a customer. Also okay: American-made beers, the Boston Red Sox (except for caps wishing Carl Yastrzemski a happy retirement).

2. T-SHIRTS: As a rule of thumb, if it's available in Old Orchard Beach during the summer, then it probably is all right. T-shirts advertising running shoes, ski equipment, out-of-state colleges, out-of-state sports teams (except the Red Sox) are no-no's. Exception: Anything from Florida, the only state that compares to Maine in the quality of its cheap merchandise.

3. T-SHIRTS FROM MAINE SUMMER FESTIVALS: It's a case-by-case basis. A guideline: Is the event designed to attract and involve Maine people or tourists? Thus, t-shirts from the Spruce Head Lobster Crate Race are Wicked Good, while those of the Maine Festival are dead ducks. SPECIAL TIP: With or without logos, sleeveless t-shirts, the "muscle shirt" of an earlier generation, are never fashionable. Trust the fashion expert on this one: Sleeveless t-shirts are one of the signals the you-know-who's use to recognize each other.

8. LIFESTYLE

Are They Wicked Good?

We asked our Panel of Experts

YES	NO	
x		Lawn ornaments
	x	Lawn mowers
	x	Saunas
x		Skinny dipping
x		Chainsaws
	x	Electric carving knives
x		Rowboats
	x	Rowing machines
x		Outhouses
	x	Clivus Multrums
	x	Septic tanks
x		Cleaning septic tanks for a living
	x	Books about how to become rich, famous or powerful
x		*The Joy of Sex*
	x	Books about how to manage your time
	x	*Hollywood Wives*
x		*Hollywood Squares*
x		Spaghetti
	x	Pasta
x		Jelly donuts
	x	Pineapples
x		Pines
x		Apples
	x	Oranges
	x	Anita Bryant
x		Florida in winter
x		*Candlepins for Cash*
	x	*Masterpiece Theatre*

UNDERSTANDING LAWN ORNAMENTS

The editors of *YankEast* Magazine have just put together in one collection those entertaining and educational articles on lawn ornaments you've come to love over the years. You'll love **Understanding Lawn Ornaments — the Maine Way.** Only $19.95. If you're a newcomer who's just exploded your first whitewall tire, or an old hand looking for additions to your collection of little Greek boys, you'll treasure every page of this fabulous collection.

Here's what you'll get!

Introduction by Barbara Bush: the Second Lady, herself a relative newcomer to lawn ornaments, describes her personal joy and satisfaction in decorating the Bush compound in Kennebunkport. You'll hear her own words how the joys of lawn ornaments have kept Mrs. Veep sane during stressful times with George.

1. Express Yourself by Harsden Martley. First published in 1942, this important article by the noted Maine black-velvet painter and father of the Flamingist School, is credited with bringing lawn ornaments to the forefront of Maine culture.

2. Lawn Ornament Do's and Don'ts, by the exterior decorating staff of *YankEast*. Step-by-step yardplans of some of the most successful ornament layouts in the state along with hints on how you can have a model yard.

3. Have Fun But Don't Get Hurt: Lawn Ornament Safety. Never drink the water in the bird bath and other light-hearted, yet instructional tips.

Bonsai Flamingoes

This Wicked Good resident tastefully hides his radar dish by the use of two ceramic deer. Many neighbors have been so taken by the painted tractor tire that they have not noticed the dish at all.

4. Bonsai Flamingoes — *The Ancient Oriental Art of Indoor Ornaments.* Flamingoes one inch high? Plastic butterflies the size of ... butterflies? Gazing balls the size of marbles? The secret of this amazing oriental art — in photographs.

5. Wall Butterflies —*Ornaments or Not: The Debate Rages.* You decide as two young ornamentalists discuss this burning issue.

6. Handcrafted Ornaments. The economical alternatives you can make at home, by the staff of *YankEast.*

   Clorox bottles

   "Cats, cats, cats"

   Contemporary Maine whirligigs:

      Truck dumping toxic waste

      Yuppie eating cheese

7. The Future, by the *YankEast* staff:

   Ornament dancing

   Ornament modelling

Ornament mime

Ornament garb

Ornament punk

Ornaments and the microchip

Wicked Good Landscaping

Don't delay. Order your copy of *Understanding Lawn Ornaments — the Maine Way* while supplies last!

PINK FLAMINGOES
(to the tune of *The Unicorn Song*)

Late last spring when the lawn turned green
I moved the skidder and the snow machine.
I moved the old Sears dryer and all the other culch too.
I had to make room for the Ornament Zoo.

CHORUS:
There were Pink Flamingoes and concrete geese;
Some elves under mushrooms and cats in the trees;
Some painted saints and butterflies and little Greek boys too —
But there were no chipmunks in the Ornament Zoo.

Mother came out of the mobile home;
Through the front and back yard she started to roam.
She liked the tires round the driveway, she liked the gazin' ball too.
But she really had her heart set on a chipmunk for the Ornament Zoo.

CHORUS

I went back into the trailer and got my hamster Paul.
I dipped him in some quick-dry cement and I heaved him on the wall.
Mother was so happy, she sort of liked where he flew.
Now she's got a semichipmunk in the Ornament Zoo.

Right there with Pink Flamingoes and concrete geese;
Elves under mushrooms and cats in the trees;
Some painted saints and butterflies and little Greek boys too.
Now she can't cuss at me no more 'cause she's finally got herself
a chipmunk in the Ornament Zoo.

WICKED GOOD ARCHITECTURE

Simulated wood-grain siding and gas bottles are sure signs of distinctive architecture in the Wicked Good Style.

Exterior accessories are important in completing the Wicked Good look. Here we see the careful placement of ceramic cats to offset the symmetrical balance of the upper-story windows.

Energy-conscious Mainers use this special aluminum siding with an R-factor of minus 4.

It's always good to have a guest house for when the in-laws come to visit.

Non-Wicked Good Architecture: This Federalist facade represents the chaotic state of architecture that existed before the Wicked Good Era. One can still see a few remaining examples in culturally isolated areas around the state.

Velma's HOUSE OF CASSEROLES

Brrringg.

"Hello, Velma's House of Casseroles. May I help you?"

"Yes, I'd like to order the tuna, pea, noodle and baco bits."

"Okay. Which size would you like — Honeymooners, In-Laws' Surprise, The Whole Gang, or Church Supper?"

"In-Laws."

"Yeah, I thought so. The tuna 'n' pea is usually good for in-laws."

"Can you deliver?"

"If the Buick is working, we'll bring it over at six. Thanks for calling."

Brrringg.

"Hello. Velma's House of Casseroles."

"Hi, honey, how's it going?"

"Oh, about average for a Thursday. Three or four Tupperware parties and the advance orders for church suppers. Which reminds me, can you bring over a couple of large cans of cream of mushroom soup? The Nazarenes are having a New Members

Industrial-Strength Casserole In A Drum

Here's a great idea for when you've got to feed the whole gang — and you know they'll eat anything. Velma's, famous for innovative culinary delights, presents the recipe for its all-purpose, all-ingredient taste treat. Starred items* are trademark products of Velma's Kitchens and are available at selected Maine stores.

- 5 lbs Otter Dogs* (Made from the whole of the otter — you "otter try 'em")
- 5 lbs generic dark tuna in oil
- 5 lbs Baco-Drip* (just like Sunday mornin' drippin's)
- 5-1-lb boxes generic macaroni & cheese
- 1 can cream-style corn
- 5 lbs cottage cheese with chives
- 5 lbs "aged" Maine potatoes - rocks and all
- 5 lbs Velma-Veeta* cheese (made in the vats of U.S. Steel)
- 1 big bottle of ketchup
- 1 jar cocktail olives
- 1 kid-size box of cornflakes

Cut the Otter Dogs into ⅜" pieces and fry in the Baco-Drip. Melt the Velma-Veeta cheese on the exhaust pipe of your car. Add the tuna, the cottage cheese and half the bottle of ketchup. Take a chain saw and cut up the potatoes. Grease up a 6-foot-length of culvert with the rest of the Baco-Drip. Cook it on your mother-in-law's woodstove the next time she goes to Rumford for a couple of days. For a festive touch, slice up the olives and the corn flakes in your Veg-O-Matic and sprinkle them on top. Pour the rest of the ketchup on each serving to drown out the taste. Serves an entire church supper on Saturday night.

Night."

"Sure. What's for dinner tonight?"

"I'm bringing home the American chop suey I made for the Seventh-Day Adventists. They didn't tell me they were vegetarians, and I loaded the hamburg to it."

"You mean the mystery meat, don't ya?"

"Russell, if you even breathe a word about that to the wrong people, I'll be out of business. And you'll be singing soprano on Sunday morning."

"Don't worry, honey, I wanna keep the family jewels."

"Look, I've got to go. There's a customer in here. Bye-bye."

"Yes. May I help you?"

"Hi. I'm doing a Wicked Good Theme Party on the nineteenth. I understand you can put the whole thing together."

"Ayuh, from the lawn ornaments to the potato bobbing. And I even sing with the band."

"Well, how about the food? I want the otter dog and scallop potatoes, the tuna wiggle, and the strawberry jello salad. But there are some people who aren't from Maine. Do you have any quiche?"

"Look, Buster, I run a clean operation here. There are laws against that sort of thing."

"Hey, I'm sorry, okay? No quiche. Can you deliver this thing on a skidder?"

"Now your're talking. No problem. I'll be there with bells on..."

Brrringg.

"Excuse me. Hello, Velma's House of Casseroles."

"Good morning. This is the Methodist Conference of New England. We're putting bean suppers out to bid for all eight hundred twenty-one Methodist churches in the region for all year. Your name has been highly recommended several times."

"Oh, my God. I mean, yes... The birds in the mail. I mean, the bid's in the mail... Thank you so much. Good-bye."

"Was that good news?"

"Better than winning a lottery ticket and Ten-Card Beano Sweeps on the same day. I guess we're all set for your Wicked Good Party on the nineteenth?"

"Can you get the-ah from he-ah?"

"Oh, you're so funny! I'll see you then."

Dial—Dial—Dial

"Hello."

"Russell? Let's go out shopping tonight for that Bessemer process giant bean cauldron. We're gonna need it."

Velma's PRODUCTS

Leave it to that darn Velma. She'll come up with more products than a Junior Achievement club. She knows what Maine people want — quality at a fair price. And she knows that Maine people never get what they want, so they'll have to settle for shoddy quality at inflated prices.

VELMAMINTS — Make your breath smell just like you've eaten an Italian Sandwich with extra onions. One handful of Velmamints will let you know who your friends are.

VELMA-VEETA CHEESE - The steel mills of Pittsburgh and the shoe shops of Lewiston are together at work once again in the manufacture of industrial-process Velma-Veeta cheese. Now available in 6-foot by 8-foot sizes for paneling.

VELMA-SOL DETERGENT— No time to clean the trailer and your mother-in-law is coming over in 15 minutes? Just open up a bottle of VELMA-SOL and let its fumes waft about the house. People will think you have been doing spring cleaning all day. Also available: "First Day of School" Odor for school boards on a budget. Why hire a cleaning crew for the whole summer when you can open up a "First Day" drum!

VELMA-WRAP — From last night's fish to tomorrow's lunch, everything goes better in Velma-Wrap. We've taken some of Maine's most prestigious daily and weekly newspapers and put them in an easy-to-wrap format. Handy for starting the woodstove, too.

VELMIUM — Having trouble saying "not tonight, I've got a headache"? Modern science has come up with the answer: a pill that will give you a headache in minutes! Velma herself has used this with her first three husbands. Good for bringing those boring parties to a quick end, too. NO prescription needed.

You Need A Haircut

Bob's Barber Shop

You need a haircut. Oh sure, you just spent seventeen dollars down at Mainely Manes Hair Stylists for a shampoo, razor cut and blow dry. You were served almond-flavored coffee in a mug with little seals on it by the receptionist, a former Miss Maine Poultry Products, while you were waiting for Mandy, your stylist. You read *Playboy* and *GQ* while you were in the chair and now you look, feel and act like a contestant on *Dance Fever*.

But this is Maine and you need a haircut.

Forget your appearance for a minute, because getting a haircut is much more than that. To say that a haircut in Maine is just for appearance's sake is like saying that salmon fighting upstream to spawn is just another swim. No, it's much more than that.

If you want a Maine haircut and all that goes with it, follow these two simple rules: 1) If the name of the place where you are going to get your haircut does not contain the name of the guy who is going to cut your hair, go somewhere else. 2) If the guy who is going to cut your hair is not a guy at all, but a girl, go somewhere else.

Take, for instance, Bob Feeney's Barber Shop in Portland. Bob is the barber to the Wicked Good and the near Wicked Good...has been for thirty years. The authors of this book spent hours of their youth sitting in Bob's chair. And it wasn't a canvas deck chair like you'll find at the stylist's. It was, and is, a real barber chair.

On any Saturday morning, there are more white-walls inside Bob's shop than there are going by on Allen Avenue.

Bob's taste runs heavily into the *Argosy*, *Field & Stream*, and *Popular Mechanics* end of the literary spectrum. He always has a fair supply of comic books. There are lots of ashtrays around, men's ash-trays — little tires with the ashtrays in the middle. There are no signs that say "Thank you for not smoking."

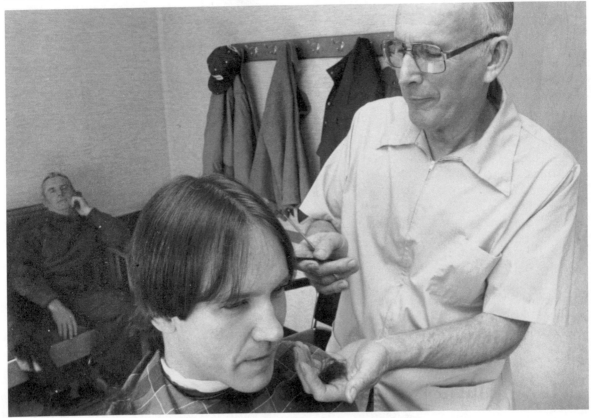

Bob Feeney's Barber Shop on a typical Saturday morning.

Frig, You Say?

"'Frig,' you say? Well, I recollect back in the fifth grade, and I'm sure it was the fifth grade because that was the year we lived over on the Rockland Road, in the fifth grade we had a teacher named Mrs. Rudman. Now she had been a teacher for a good many years, probably at least as many years as that old school building had been there, and I should know because my father and his sisters all had Mrs. Rudman when they were in the fifth grade, too, and they were in it three years running each. I'd have to say she was pretty old by the time I had her. She had some bulging bridgework and gray hair streaked with white, and she wore the same two print dresses, each a faded grayish print, all year long. I don't think there was a Mr. Rudman, or not much left of him anyway, so Mrs. Rudman was sort of the same as being an old maid. Mrs. Rudman never used dirty words in front of the class, I'm sure it was, because in addition to being a school teacher she went to church every week, at least that's what Lyman Moody told me. She used to stand there at the blackboard during arithmetic lessons and the flaps of skin underneath her elbows would bang against the blackboard, creating a big cloud of dust, the same kind of dust you'd see coming off her elbow flap when she put her coat on to take us out to the playground. Well, one morning — and it had to be morning because that was when we had arithmetic, just after we had the little bottles of milk that had been setting out back until they were lukewarm — one morning she was showing us how to do long division. She had a long new piece of chalk, and she was using it to write a big number divided by a smaller number, and as she went on the upstroke the chalk broke and it screeched against the blackboard, which caused considerable consternation, especially among some of the girls who liked to be upset by such things. Well, you remember how I said that Mrs. Rudman never used dirty words? That time the chalk broke, she said, loud, but not too loud: 'Frig, F-R-I-G.' That's right: she even spelled it out, like it was a spelling bee. Anyway, I would have to say that if Old Mrs. Rudman, who was a practically unviolated lady and a church-goer, could spell it out to her fifth-grade class, the word 'frig' just wasn't a dirty word..."

BOWDOINHAM
COLLEGE

Catologue

70

President's office

A Word From The President — Vinal Jacket

Welcome to Bowdoinham College, a unique experience for a young person who wants to while away his or her hours while waiting to grow up. Since 1971, we've tried, but not too hard, to provide an atmosphere that reflects the "real Maine": mediocre education and a general indifference to the way things turn out. The Bowdoinham experience has become a tradition in its short existence, and if you think you're going to change it, you're barking up the wrong tree, bub.

You'll find the campus, the activities, and the other students just the way you like them. If you don't, you probably don't belong here.

As President of this college I wear many hats. The one I like best is the red-and-black-checked woolen one with the black ear flaps. Of course, besides being President, I maintain contact with the academic life. I teach the fall semester class in kerosene barrel repair and the spring semester seminar in advanced carbohydrate loading.

So have a brew, light up a joint, turn on the tube and read this catalogue to the best of your ability. And as you are reading, keep our motto in mind: *Qui Faecem Donat?*

History of Bowdoinham College

Great changes were occurring in the academic world in the year 1971. Campus revolts of the 1960s had forced colleges to address the needs of their students, not just academic needs. Many colleges catered to smart kids; other colleges started up for disadvantaged kids. The glaring need appeared for a college to serve mediocre students of average means. A debate raged in the academic administrative world between those who favored "liberal" campuses, where anything went, and "conservative" campuses, with their rigid lifestyles.

Here in Bowdoinham, the debate was resolved when some back-to-the-landers got crossed with some dyed-in-the-wool locals, and the result was the first class at Bowdoinham College. Bowdoinham's student body was once described as being "hippies and rednecks at the same time." The tradition of Bowdoinham Boys was born. Even the women are proud, as much as they are proud of anything, of being Bowdoinham Boys.

Student Body

Ask anyone how to get to Bowdoinham College and they'll tell you: "Study — but not too hard." We have tried to keep the rich diversity of America out of Bowdoinham. Our students come from two states, Maine and Ohio (someone lied on their application). To be more truly reflective of Maine people, however, we do have differences in such important groups as hair color (black or brown), hunting shirt color (red or green), and length of beard (long or wicked long). While all religions are practiced (Sunday cartoon watcher, Methodist, Congregationalist), none is favored. We even let the priest from Brunswick come over and do his papist mumbo-jumbo once a week. Our students are just like kids anywhere in college, we guess. We'd tell you more, but we can't figure out how to use statistics, and who cares anyway?

Academics

We don't have too much in the way of academics. You don't have to be very smart to get by in Maine, anyway. Instead we load up on the technical, the how-to courses. Here are some of the courses for the coming year.

American Studies (This Year's Topic: Dope vs. Beer)
Archaeology in an Ashtray
Biology 122 — Road Kill Dissection
Basic Canadian
Diesel Fume Management
Education 316 — Ignorance Then and Now
Energy Topics — Woodstoves for Non-Yuppies
Engineering 207 — The Frost Heave
Engineering 310 — Nukular Power
French III (Prerequisite — French IV)
Fly Tying
Fly Zipping
Fly Buttoning
Fly Spraying
History 061 — The History of Beer
Japanese Car Destruction
Classics Illustrated I
Classics Illustrated II
Philosophy 12 — Epistemology of Beer
Philosophy 14 — Logic of the Pothead Group
Spanish Fly Tying

Sex Education for Non-Preverts
Theology 117 — How to Watch Cartoons on Sunday Morning
Theology 666 — Church Defacing Then and Now

Student Life

We do what we can to make student life like it should be in the real world. That's why Bowdoinham College presents a well-rounded program of food experiences and activities.

Food: Our food is designed around the expected day of a Bowdoinham student:

11:30-11:35 AM — BREAKFAST: Your choice of Beer and Rice Krispies, Beer and Jelly Donuts, or Fried Spam and Beer, all washed down with a giant pot of Mr. Mud Coffee.

12:00-12:22 PM — DINNER: Usually Fried "Special Harvest" Clams, Road Squab, or Deer Meat and Gravy over White Bread served with your choice of Regular or Lite Beer.

5:30-5:31 PM — SUPPER: A combination of what's left from Breakfast and Dinner, along with Turnip Surprise, Tripe Pizza, Twinkies and a pitcher of Beer.

6-12 PM — MUNCHIE TIME: "Special" Brownies (the kind that make you hungry for more), "Special" Cookies, "Special" Ice Cream Bars, and Beer.

The campus

Organizations

You'll find a small number of clubs that might be of interest to you, if you are interested in anything. The number of clubs is small because everybody has about the same interests, and it's too much of a hassle to get organized and do stuff. But you may find some enjoyment in the Young Carpenters Club which is building a log cabin out of the Bowdoinham Pines which were clearcut last year by the Skidder Club.

The Beer Club has a worthwhile project for the school year: "Beer for Ethiopia." They are saving all empty cans which they will cash in at the end of the year and send six-packs to the drought-stricken country. The Forest Fire Club is planning a summer trip to Baxter State Park where they will try out a few experiments. And the Intercollegiate Raking Crew sponsors competitions with other colleges.

Athletics

Men and Women Beer Teams
Women's Mud Wrestling
Skidder Basketball
Men's Varsity Hunkerball
Varsity and JV Sleep Teams

Our hockey rink

Spring Break

Every year, Bowdoinham Boys find sun, sea and excitement during spring break. A great number of them catch the rays and fun at the Commercial Street Beach in Portland.

Just relaxin' and waitin' for the tide to roll in

A stroll on the Boardwalk

Surf's up! Time for a swim

74

Admissions Info

Unlike many colleges, Bowdoinham College does not require College Boards. If you can pass a couple of two-by-fours over your head, you will probably do okay. Have your sister or the guy who sells you beer fill out the following application.

NAME (As you would like it spelled on your diploma):

_____

NICKNAME:_____ AGE: _____ SEX?: _____ (yes) _____(no)

LAST KNOWN ADDRESS: _____

KIND OF BEER YOU DRINK: _____ Lite _____ Reg. _____ Canadian _____ Other _____

NO. OF SIX-PACKS YOU DRINK PER DAY: _____ (If less than 2, why?) _____

BRAND YOU SMOKE: _____ ___Filter ___Unfiltered ___Mexican ___Homegrown_____

ACADEMIC EXPERIENCE: Explain all grades in high school that were higher than C: _____

_____

THINGS YOU DID BESIDES SCHOOL: _____

_____

_____

_____

ESSAY: DESCRIBE HUNTING SHIRT: _____ ___ Red ___ Green.

ESSAY: DESCRIBE BEARD (If a girl, describe a beard you like): _____

LIST ALL TRAFFIC VIOLATIONS: _____

_____

_____

_____

ARE YOU REALLY FROM MAINE? _____ DO YOU: _____ Snore? _____ Use Right Guard?

_____ Eat Twinkies? _____ Pick your teeth with your pencil? _____ Have teeth? _____

When you have completed this application, have your parents send $1,972.50, or 3 months' food stamps, to: Bowdoinham College, Dump Road, Bowdoinham, Maine.

10. WICKED GOOD PEOPLE

The Wyeths of Cushing, Maine

Me 'n' Andy live in a big ol' drafty farmhouse. I ask him hundreds of times why he don't want to live in a trailer like other folks. He says this house helps his integrity, whatever that means. And he gets that look about him when I ask him a question that he thinks is dumb. Like when I was askin' him about the trailer. I hinted that Pa 'n' Ma might like to move their trailer out to the back field. I says it would be easier for me to visit Ma, and Ma could come over and visit me, 'cause after all *he* don't spend hardly any time with me.

Not that Andy is out doin' anything like working. He just sets around the house and "paints." The first time I told Ma that he was a painter, she says to me, "Just like the cobbler's son that ain't got shoes, and the miller's kid ain't got bread." I think she meant by that that our house was the most unpainted in the whole town. What paint was left was peelin' real bad. My brother-in-law, Dougie Laffin, tried to come over one time and sell Andy some vinyl sidin', but Andy starts mumbling some-thing about the integrity of the structure. And Ma, she's always tryin' to help out. She rummaged up a couple of house jobs for Andy to do. Sure, they was just little houses, and one they wanted sort of bright blue, but Andy turns his nose up at them. He shouts about "artistic integrity." Then he shuts himself in the front parlor and don't come out for nearly two days.

I get tired of the cars turnin' in the driveway all the time, crunchin' the gravel and runnin' over the marigold bed I planted next to the little wishing well. The other day I put a sign up about no turnin' in the driveway, but I guess *some people* can't read good or somethin'. A big Lincoln pulls up in the driveway, crunchin' the rocks, and then it starts beepin', beepin', actually blastin' away on its big ol' horn. I'm in the middle of *Days of Our Lives*, and Andy is busy with his integrity somewhere, but finally I figure if I don't see what it is I'll never get peace. So I get up and go out into the dooryard just in time to hear the beepin', beepin' again. A guy

ARE THEY WICKED GOOD?

Is Wicked Good	Ain't
Billy Carter	Jimmy Carter
Elvis Presley (pre-1965)	Elvis Costello
Daniel Boone	Pat Boone
Tex Ritter	John Ritter
People named "Bud"	People Named "Buffy"
Jerry Lewis	Jerry Falwell
People who like Andre the Seal	Andre the Seal
Walter Brennan	Joe Brennan
Tip O'Neill	Ryan O'Neal

ARE YOU WICKED GOOD?

Let our Panel of Experts decide.
Send $10 to: Wicked Good Panel
Corsica, Maine

The judges will use the following checklist:

Did the person send the ten bucks?

Yes _____   No _____

If you are found to be Wicked Good, you will not be notified, since if you are truly Wicked Good it won't make any difference. If you are found to be non-Wicked Good, you will not be notified, since it won't make any difference to us.

rolls down the window and says, "Where's Christina's world?" Now I got an idea what he might be talkin' about, but I want to make sure. "Christina who?" I says, and I look right at him.

"Olson. Mrs. Olson," he says.

"Why, is that the Mrs. Olson on the coffee commercial on TV?"

Now the guy is mad. I can tell, 'cause his face is red as an old radish. He says: "Is this or is this not the home of the Wyeths."

I says: "It depends on which Wyeths you mean."

"The artist Wyeths, if you must know," he says with such an air of "I know about all there is to know." I want to tell him if he knows it all he can know where these artists live.

"Well," I says, "there's Vinal Wyeth, who's a lobster fisherman by day, but he can whittle a mean decoy. Then there's Wanda Wyeth, whose multicolor jello salads have received rave reviews at Methodist suppers for years..." He started splutterin' sort of like a lawnmower runnin' out of gas... "There's N.C. Wyeth," I continued. "He used to be an illustrator. Then there's Andy, who's a painter, but he don't do lighthouses. And of course, Jamie, but he can't stand it out here in the sticks." As the Lincoln driver starts to open his mouth, I cut him off. "And there's one more Wyeth who has done a fair share of art work."

"Who's that?" he says.

"Me. I'm Waynette Wyeth, and I painted that sign that you nearly knocked over, the one that says no turnin' in the driveway. Now if you know what's good for you and you don't want me to do a little artwork on the grill of your car with my shotgun, you'd better turn around and head back up the road."

Like I told the man in the Lincoln, Andy don't do lighthouses. Integrity is one thing, being a damn fool is another. If you live in Maine and you paint pitchers, then you gotta do lighthouses. That's

Waynette's World

how all the artists in Maine make their livin'. I don't know how many times I told this to Andy, but he gives me one of them mind-your-own-beeswax sniffs, and says he ain't gonna do lighthouses, even if you can get fifty bucks from the tourists who stop at the Texaco Station in Thomaston looking for stuff to buy. It ain't only lighthouses he don't do. Ma, she don't give up on tryin' to help, so when she found out he wouldn't paint houses but was paintin' pitchers, she drags over two kittens and three assorted grandkids. She plunks 'em down in the kitchen and announces: "I ain't leavin' till Andy does a pitcher of one or all of 'em."

"Ma," I cry, "he ain't gonna. This integrity business is drivin' him nuts."

But before I can say any more, she says, "and I want the kids done with big eyes. Now that's the kind of pitcher people are gonna buy."

She sets there in the chair, creakin' back and forth for two hours. Andy walks through a couple of times and just glares at her, the kids, the cats, and me. Pretty soon the kids get hungry, and I ain't gonna feed 'em, 'cause they won't touch the quiche I gotta make for Andy. So they leave, and Ma says, "I'll be back." And I say: "Take your time."

You can't blame Ma and Pa and the relatives for tryin' to help. It's just their nature. But it works me up when Andy starts sniffin' and fussin'. I says to him just before he goes on one of his trips to New York, "How come you gotta go to New York to sell pitchers, when everybody from New York comes here in the summer and they'll buy 'em in the summertime?" I could have predicted an "integrity" speech, and he don't let me down, sayin' something about integrity of the artist's relation to the public. It's all B.S., if you pardon my French...

It's movin' day, and I ain't going. Not that I was asked, but I probably wouldn't of gone anyway. I didn't find out about it until yesterday, when Andy tells me he's going to Pennsylvania for a while, some place called Chad's Ford.

Now I don't know who this Chad is, and I don't want to know. There was so much talk when they showed that pitcher Andy done of the naked boy. When Pa seen that he wanted to break Andy in two, but Ma stopped him. She thought maybe she could get a deal on a hairdo or somethin'. Andy certainly don't do hair. That wouldn't fit his integrity, either.

There's been too much talk anyway, with some people claimin' they could make better pitchers with a Polaroid camera, and others, like the snooty Ladies Aid at the church, sayin' they don't like the pitchers of houses with dingy curtains.

Well, he can take his "integrity" and shove it, 'cause I got better things to do than listen to someone sniffin' all day. Still, someday I'll probably miss the talks we had over the TV dinners, and I'll miss the big ol' drafty house, with the smell of paint thinner waftin' through every room...

And the view from the window I'll kinda miss, too, the one of that Olson woman always crawlin' toward the house.

DEAR DUBBY

Dr. Dubby Flanders, Sociology Professor at the Governor John Reed Institute of Charisma, answers your personal questions.

DEAR DUBBY: I am concerned about my sixteen-year-old son. Kevin has always been a good student and has always helped out around our family farm. But a few weeks ago, I found him smuggling one of our sheep into his bedroom late at night. When I asked him what he was doing, he told me that he heard the sheep sneeze several times and didn't want it to get seriously ill. It seemed like his typical thoughtfulness, so I let the sheep stay.

The problem is, Dubby, the sheep has been there ever since. The last straw came a few nights ago when I went into his bedroom to tuck him in and I found the two of them together in his bed, smoking cigarettes. Kevin told me he was doing a 4H project on the effects of cigarette smoke on farm animals. Dubby, I don't know what to think. I want to trust him.

Baa-wildered in East Baldwin

DEAR BAA-WILDERED: Trust is always important in a parent-teenager relationship, but you should squash this before it turns into something Kevin can't handle. Talk to Kevin and try to point out the seriousness of what he is doing. If he continues, have him talk with your family minister and, if even that doesn't make him stop, make an appointment for him with your family physician. Maybe the sight of some X-rays of cancerous lungs will prove to him that smoking is nothing to fool around with.

78

DEAR DUBBY: Don't get me wrong: I love my husband. But I'm going to go crazy if we can't clear this situation up. Orin (not his real name) and I have gone to church together every Sunday that we've been married — that's twenty-three years. Some time in the last four or five years, Orin's nose has started whistling all through the service. Dubby, he breathes through his nose most of the time and it never whistles outside of church. At first I thought it was just coincidental that it always happened in church. But lately, he's been whistling "Lo, My Shepherd is Divine" through the entire service. Dubby, I'm embarrassed and ashamed, what should I do?

Embarrassed Baptist in Baldwin

DEAR EMBARRASSED: Orin has what is known as a Diviniated Septum. More common in ancient times (in fact, before the advent of the pipe organ, congregations would have all members with diviniated septums accompany the choir on all hymns), it is now a rare, totally inexplicable gift. It should be cherished. Talk with your pastor and try to arrange a special part of each service for Orin to solo. For example, he could whistle the doxology.

DEAR DUBBY: My first wife passed away nearly two years ago, when the number-ten curlers she was wearing were struck by lightning while we were standing in line at the frozen custard stand. I thought I would never get over her. But six months ago, Dubby, I met another woman and I think I'm in love again. Dorcas (not her real name) has almost succeeded in making me forget the bad taste left in my mouth from the incident at the frozen custard stand. I want to marry her, but there's one problem.

You see, what attracted me to Dorcas was what attracted me to my first wife — a beehive hairdo. But in order to get the "look" I love, she says she has to wear number-ten curlers. I wouldn't love her without the beehive and I don't know if I can risk losing another loved one to an electrical storm. What should I do?

Beehive Blues in Baldwin

DEAR BEEHIVE: A simple groundwire, the kind you might find on the TV antenna on your roof, run from the curlers to the ground, is enough to solve the problem. If she doesn't love you enough to ground those curlers, take her out for frozen custard at the first sight of a black cloud in the west.

Cabin Fever

The worst time of year is not the dead of winter. It's not the slop of mud season. And it's not the torture of black fly and tourist time. The worst time is "t'aint." I call it that because it t'aint winter and t'aint mud season. It's the time we get the most wicked case of Cabin Fever.

Winter's just about had it. You can't go out on the ice in the Blazer any more. You sent the old lady out last week, and she started sinking in, so you wouldn't be trusting the vehicle. That makes it no good for smelting. You couldn't get the cabin out there even if you wanted to. All the empties you had been saving to cash in for a smeltin' party went for a new set of trunions on the Dodge.

And being inside isn't all that great neither. You got tired of checkers last week. Much as you love cribbage, that marathon cribbage tourney two weekends ago left you with a desire to put the board up for a while. The wife was working on a one-thousand-piece jigsaw puzzle, but the cat peed on the thing and you had to set it outside.

I'd have to say there's something about the odor of the cabin that creates the fever. Of course, it could be because of that spaghetti dinner last January that neither you nor she cleaned up after.

The things that once were endearing to you now can drive you stark crazy. Like her gurgling stomach. It used to be just the cutest thing to hear it bubbling away, kind of like a clogged-up bath tub slowly draining out. But, you know, when you're just sitting there and you're trying to concentrate on the captions of that *Sports Illustrated* bathing suit issue, just as a sort of excuse to keep the pages open, and the gurgling comes on, so loud that it nearly knocks you out of the La-Z-Boy, and you know she just ate an hour ago, you get to grumbling. "Cheryl Tiegs don't have a gurgling stomach," you might say, real quiet.

"What?" she says.

"Oh, nothing."

But then later, you're listening to the scanner. You've brought in two planes at the Jetport. You've made a couple of arrests for drunk driving and one for going through a speed trap without a fuzz buster. You're closing in on the 10-20 of the warden who's out looking for illegal deer meat. He's about to give away his location when ... the gurgle obliterates every other sound in the room,

A sure sign Cabin Fever Season is over: The ice breaks up. Sometimes this doesn't happen until July.

rattles the windows, even causes a big clump of snow to come off the roof and to land on top of the Willys.

"Jeezus H. Baldheaded Christ!"

"What's wrong, dear?"

"Oooh, nothing." The worst part of the whole thing is that you have to hold your tongue on such a matter. Because if you say one thing that's the least bit critical, it's like putting a match to tinder that's been soaked in kerosene. If you start things off, there's bound to be a return comment. She'll comment on how a colony of field mice is starting a nest in the middle of that pile of *Field and Stream* magazines in the shed. To which you will respond that you can remember last week when you were shaving and your razor blade touched that pink box full of highly charged pink rollers and you nearly got fried like a strip of bacon...and what do you need your hair up and why do you have to smell the house up like a beauty salon when there ain't nobody gonna see you besides those old hens in your bowling league who look more like they need a trip to the poodle parlor!

But you don't say anything. It's a test of nerves, and it's a test of endurance. The first one that fails the test has to stay in the doghouse for the duration of the winter, and it's mighty cold out there.

Instead, you learn how to mutter, and you think of clever things that you don't intend to say to her face. And you vow to save all your returnables for a whole year so that next year about this time you can get a ticket to Florida like half of the other people in the state do.

For this year, you try to content yourself with a thought: The ice cover on the lake is just about melted. Somewhere under that ice, the biggest salmon in the entire state is taking a nap. But he's gonna be waking up in just a few weeks. And you're gonna find him. He's gonna fight just enough to make it a hard-won battle. But you're gonna win that battle. Just the thought of that salmon, cooking up on your stove, makes your stomach gurgle in perfect harmony with hers. You're going to make it through the Cabin Fever Season once again. But just barely.

Generic towns dot the Maine map.

11. WICKED GOOD PLACES

Mr. Libby's Neighborhood

"It's a wonderful day to be Wicked Good..."

Hi there, boys and girls, and welcome to Mr. Libby's Neighborhood. Mr. Libby lives in Maine, where people say things like "ayuh" and "wicked good." Can you say "ayuh"? Can you say "wicked good"?

This is Ballantine Ale. Can you say "Bally Ale"? This is a pack of Lucky Strikes. Can you say "Luckies"? Good. Go to the store and get me a six-pack of Bally Ale and a carton of Luckies.

Today we're going to go aboard Mr. Libby's lobster boat. Do you know how to catch a lobster? First you have to get some friggin' bait. Can you say "friggin' bait"? Then you have to make sure the CB radio is working okay. Can you say "ten fowah"? Then you have to bring your shotgun in case someone is trying to move into your territory. Do you know how to use a shotgun? Good. Fire a couple of volleys over the head of that guy over to Spruce Point. He's getting too close to my buoys.

Now we're coming up to our traps. Let's pull them in and see what we've got. Oops, looks like someone has cut our line. Can you say "god-damned trawler"? Now, here's one line with a trap on it. Look at those lobsters squirming around in there. They aren't red, like you see on your plate. They're kind of black. They only get red after they get boiled. You would get red too if you got boiled. Would you like to be boiled? No?

I'm putting bait in this trap to catch more lobsters. Did you wonder why I didn't put bait in the last trap over there? That's because I'm going after a different kind of catch — can you say "mara-hoochie"? Well, I can't say it very good either, but I know that when I get a trap full of it, and when I bring it over to MacVane's wharf and leave it, there are no questions asked. Then I can get enough money to make a down payment on a new boat. Can you say "friggin' old tub"? I have been saying that for a few too many years to worry about what I am catching.

It's time now to go home for supper. Can you say "chowdah"? What do you mean you've said it every day this week? Why don't you go for a swim out to Barter's Island at high tide? Oh, you decided you liked chowdah, did you?

Here we are now at the dock, where we'll unload the lobsters and drink our beer. Can you drink beer? Of course you can, as long as it isn't my beer you're drinking. And you can smoke a pipe, too, just like me. Now can you say "ayuh"? Well, I guess you still need a little more practice. Maybe in about twenty years you'll begin to get the hang of it.

It's time for Mr. Libby to take off his yellow oil slicker and put on his comfy wool shirt and go home to Mrs. Libby. Maybe tomorrow we can go out and gather some sea moss. Did you know that sea moss looks a lot like marahoochie too? Bye Bye!

HALF LIVE AT THE HALF MOON

If you're driving up Route One in the town of Freeport,
There's a blue neon sign that says Half Moon Motor Court:
Just six shabby cabins and two rusted cars;
You've gotta bring your own bottle, 'cause they ain't got a bar.
But I always stay here 'cause the rooms are so cheap,
And I always bring a bottle to put myself to sleep.
I've been coming here steady for eight years or nine,
And I've never seen 'em turn on that "No Vacancy" sign.

CHORUS:
I'm half live at the Half Moon tonight.
Just sittin' here suckin' down Budweiser Lite,
And hopin' somebody might want to come by and start a fight.
I'm half live at the Half Moon tonight.

A rotted DeSoto sets outside the door
Sinkin' into the ground since 1964.
And a '58 Mercury is two cabins away —
Just like me that Merc has seen its better days.
The flashing light buzzes, the cars and trucks roar by;
The TV is busted, my beer can just went dry.
But there's a store down the road just a mile or two.
Think I'll go get me another six-pack and forget about you.

CHORUS

Someday some New Yorker born with a golden spoon
Is gonna take over the lovely Half Moon.
He'll tow the DeSoto and tear down everything.
And he'll prob'ly put up an outlet and sell quiche — or some damn thing.
But 'til then you'll find me in cabin number four
Right next to the DeSoto with the two-tone green door.
Better bring along some fly dope if you come in June,
And a bottle for sleeping here at the old Half Moon.

CHORUS

BANGOR

We feel sorry for Bangor. It's a city that deserves to have an inferiority complex, even if it doesn't have one. No one from away can pronounce its name right. Somehow, it always ends up "Bangur." When a B movie is playing in the area and a TV ad is called for, the announcer at the end will say, "playing now in Ellsworth and Brewer. Coming soon to the Bangur Drive-In." Ellsworth and Brewer are little dinky towns. How come they get their name pronounced right? Recently, New England Telephone had a radio ad talking about how great your friendly local phone company was because it was installing measured rates in Portland, Lewiston and Bangur. Roger Miller's "King of the Road" featured the line "destination Bangur, Maine." They paid Willard Scott, the TV weatherman, thousands to be in a parade in Bangor, because he is the kind of person who says "Bangur," and they hoped to give him some pronunciation lessons.

SOUTH PORTLAND

South Portland is not Wicked Good. First, it stole Portland's name. Then, it stole Portland's business by starting up the Maine Mall. Then, to further the insult, when all the big oil tankers come to South Portland to unload, they spill their oil all over Portland Harbor, which is about all Portland gets out of the deal.

FRYEBURG FAIR

The Fryeburg Fair is Wicked Good. The important sights are the french fry booth, the onion ring stand, the fried sausage table, and the fudge stands. You can eat enough in one day to store up energy for an entire winter. The horse races are fun, too, if you don't bet your entire egg money. We knew a lady who used to bet on a horse depending on whether she liked the horse's name. A nag called Tuna Casserole is probably still running from last fall's race.

Whether you approve or not, there is the girlie show. We saw a woman working there who said her name was "Kitty," but who looked a lot like Miss Farnsworth, our second-grade Sunday School teacher. Kitty must have been sampling the onion rings, because her stomach kinda jiggled over the top of her bikini bottoms as she hoochie-coochied in the autumn breeze. You would have had to pay more to see more, but we felt quite sure we had seen enough.

TYPICAL MAINE TV AD

Buddy Ford Ford

Announcer: "We're talking with Buddy Ford of Buddy Ford's Ford in Biddeford. Buddy, you say 'You can't afford not to afford a beauty of a Ford at Buddy Ford's Ford in Biddeford.' Buddy, is that true?"

Buddy: "I mean it! We're changing the way cars are being sold here in the state of Maine! We got cars up the nose! And we're ready to deal! I don't care if you're Betty Ford, Ford Maddox Ford, Bjorn Borg, Deputy Dorg or live in a Norway fjord, you can't afford not to afford a beauty of a Ford at Buddy Ford's Ford in Biddeford."

Announcer: "Buddy, your fabulous Bondo deal is bringing in people from all over the state."

Buddy: "That's right! Buy a beauty of a Buddy Ford Ford at Buddy Ford's Ford in Biddeford before midnight sometime this week and get free Bondo applications for the lifetime of the car (Bondo offer not in effect where rust has occurred on the

Buddy Ford of Buddy Ford's Ford in Biddeford

surface of the vehicle's exterior). So whether you're Mary Ford, Mary Pickford, Gerry Ford, or just plain bored with your car, ford the river to Buddy Ford's Ford in Biddeford, where I say you can't afford not to afford a beauty of a Ford at Buddy Ford's Ford in Biddeford."

Lesser-Known Maine Attractions

Salem's Lot State Park

Salem's Lot State Park, Salem's Lot — The nutty, eerie world of Maine's renowned ghoulmaster, Stephen King, comes alive in this 175-acre section of a genuine Maine rural community. Picnic in Christine's garage, poke your head into Cujo's dog house (if you dare!), and check out Carrie's prom gown. Better leave Gramps at home, though. This place is wicked scary.

Le Pit-O-Maine, Le Gaz — World's largest tourmaline mine, with more than seven miles of tunnels and passageways. A special feature of Le Pit-O-Maine is its extraordinary olfactory acoustics. If someone miles away from you in the mine has been eating beans, you'll know it.

Carrabassett Hound Memorial, Bigelow Mountain — The image of these enormous but gentle dogs, battling their way through snowdrifts, with the distinctive keg of Old Lewiston Beer tied to their collars, is immediately recognizable the world over. For decades these beloved dogs have aided game wardens and ski patrols in countless rescues of lost hikers and injured skiers in Maine's rugged western mountains. This new memorial celebrates the exploits of these hardy hounds.

"Homes of the Surgeons" Tour, Portland — A twenty-minute bus tour along stately, exclusive Western Promenade and the streets between the Maine Medical Center and the posh Waynflete School. Thrill to the finest urban living modern medical science can buy.

Jungle Of Maine, the Cape — One of the geological wonders of the world. In 1878 a mysterious fissure appeared in a farmer's pasture. Within days, a thicket of dense vines, banana trees, and bamboo had overspread more than twenty acres and was still growing. Today the land, still in the same family, boasts more than four hundred species of deadly snakes and spiders, and more than three thousand other species of animals, including gorillas, elephants, and rhinos, all roaming free in their natural environment. Treat the kiddies to the popular Cobra Ride while you relax in the exclusive Apartheid Lounge.

Governor Baxter School for the Ethnic, Cumberland Foreside — When he died, Maine's most beloved philanthropist endowed this unique school. An early, primitive approach to today's concept of Wicked Good, it was Governor Baxter's dream to teach Maine's growing populations of Franco, Irish, and Italian immigrants how to talk and behave like old monied Yankees. The teaching theories developed here are now used at the Harvard Business School and at most Maine banks.

Special Exhibits this Season at the Maine State Museum, Augusta:

— From Loggers to Joggers: A Social History of Bangor.
— Beans 'Til You Turn Green: An In-depth Look at the Mores, Tools, Recipes, and Development of the Maine Bean Supper.

And don't miss:

— *The Shakier Colony*, Judgmentday Lake
— *Six Pack City*, Brewer
— *Lubec Old Poverty Days*

THE WICKED GOOD INDEX

The Degree of Wicked Goodness of a person, place or thing is subject to change because of seasonal conditions. For your better understanding of where to be, and when, here is an Index for various localities.

EASTPORT

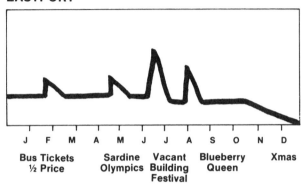

| J | F | M | A | M | J | J | A | S | O | N | D |

Bus Tickets ½ Price **Sardine Olympics** **Vacant Building Festival** **Blueberry Queen** **Xmas**

FLORIDA

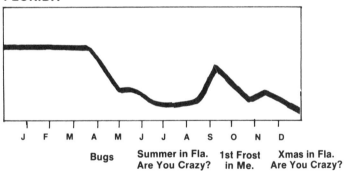

| J | F | M | A | M | J | J | A | S | O | N | D |

Bugs **Summer in Fla. Are You Crazy?** **1st Frost in Me.** **Xmas in Fla. Are You Crazy?**

LEWISTON

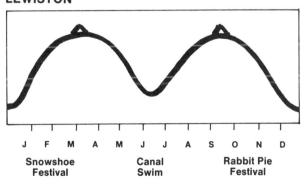

| J | F | M | A | M | J | J | A | S | O | N | D |

Snowshoe Festival **Canal Swim** **Rabbit Pie Festival**

NEW JERSEY

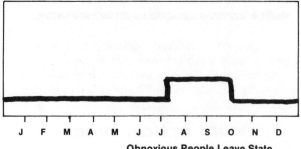

Obnoxious People Leave State,
Head for Maine

KITTERY

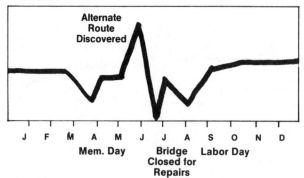

Alternate
Route
Discovered

Mem. Day   Bridge   Labor Day
            Closed for
            Repairs

HOULTON

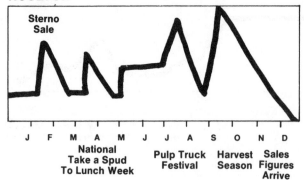

Sterno
Sale

National   Pulp Truck   Harvest   Sales
Take a Spud   Festival   Season   Figures
To Lunch Week   Arrive

GREENVILLE

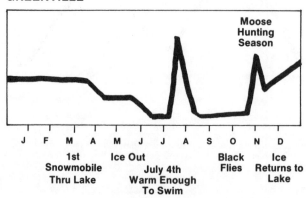

Moose
Hunting
Season

1st   Ice Out   Black   Ice
Snowmobile   Flies   Returns to
Thru Lake   July 4th   Lake
             Warm Enough
             To Swim

The Corsica Transcript Dispatch Tattler

The Only Paper In The World That Ever Covers Any News About Corsica, Maine

COUNCIL MEETING HEATS UP

The Town Council had an unusually warm session Thursday night, with the heat of the debate matching the broken thermostat that left the council chambers at a torrid 63 degrees. The council decided to award a bid for Town Hall renovations to the construction firm owned by Selectman Robert Jalbert. Jalbert told the council the repairs would enhance the building's integrity, and his firm would do the best job. "They had better do a good job. They were the highest bidder," remarked Selectman Roy Libby.

The Council also voted to approve the hiring of 20-year-old Kevin Smith as a police officer. Selectman Libby complained that Smith had been the worst juvenile driving offender in town and had been suspected of selling drugs to junior-high kids. Police Chief Ralph Smith, who is Kevin's father, told the council that "Kevin has promised to stop when he's on duty."

The council turned down a request for a rally in support of the Equal Rights Amendment after hearing opposition by Rev. Wilhelm "Billy" Crankcase of the Church of the Dour Redeemer. He said the rally would bring trouble in the form of drug addicts, pagans and homosexuals.

The council overturned a Fire Department rejection of a bonfire next Wednesday to be sponsored by the Women's Literary Society of Crankcase's church. The Rev. Crankcase cited freedom of speech and religion, as well as separation of church and state, in his demand for overturning the permit denial.

Before adjournment, Council Chairman Arthur Barker presented a gold-plated watch chain to Town Clerk Glenys Gould, who is retiring after 40 years of service. Selectman Libby asked questions about where the chain was purchased and how much it cost which we shall not report here.

HOT TIME IN THE OLD TOWN
Church Plans Bonfire, Tea

The Women's Literary Society of the Corsica Church of the Dour Redeemer has announced that next Wednesday will be "Literature Appreciation Day." Deaconesses of the Church will pour tea while various segments of "books we do not appreciate" will be read, according to WLS Chairwoman Eva Crankcase. These books will be burned at a bonfire at the High School Base-

HIGH SCHOOL NEWS

Sports Teams Excel!

The Corsica High School Heifers report great success in their sports programs. The Heifers won the State Class P Football Crown once again, thanks to the efforts of 21-year-old junior halfback "Bubba" Quimby and 20-year-old "Kahuna" Matsubeeshi. Heiffer Coach Del Viking says he'll miss the two boys next season, now that authorities have located their passports and their pro contracts have taken effect. "Kahuna" will also be missed as student coach of the Girls' Mud Wrestling Team, which is 7-2 in the Mountain Division.

Clubs

The Girls' Literary Society has pledged its support for next Wednesday's Tea and Bonfire on the baseball diamond. GLS Chairgirl Wilhelmina Crankcase met with the school librarian and asked for "all the smutty books." Librarian Doris Hurd is reviewing the request after Miss Crankcase reminded her that she had been seen in the teachers' room with a married man.

ball Field later in the day.

Mrs. Crankcase and her husband, the Rev. Wilhelm "Billy" Crankcase, have been collecting books that are "lewd, that promote unchristian lifestyles, or that preach disrespect for the fatherland," according to the Rev. Crankcase. Books to be burned include those written by "suspected homosexuals, Communists, foreigners, and those who don't believe in one true salvation."

Lighting the first match will be the Crankcase daughter, Wilhelmina. The Junior Gospel-Aires will sing "clean, appropriate, American" songs for the event, according to Crankcase.

Academics

Heifers moving on to greener pastures include: John Smith, Generic University; Kevin Pratt, Hussey School of Taxidermy; Velma Jordan (waiting list) Chuck's School of Oil Burner Repair (correspondence division). With all of these kids going on to higher education, whose gonna call us Corsicans dummies anymore, huh?

$8-MILLION PROJECT CONTINUES

The $8-million expansion project at Corsica's Church of the Dour Redeemer continues on target, according to Rev. Wilhelm "Billy" Crankcase. The air strip for Crankcase's private jet is nearly complete, and work has begun on the waste-to-energy book incinerator which is expected to supply the electricity for the TV station which will run fundraising ads to try to collect the $8 million.

88

REPORT FROM AUGUSTA

*by State Rep.
Armand Cuisinart*

A lot of lobbyists, a lot of speeches, and a lot of votes were reported around the State Capitol this week. I didn't hear too many of the speeches; I hired a guy to vote for me; and I just had the lobbyists leave their money in my post-office box. I was busy with one of my constituents this week, the Rev. Wilhelm "Billy" Crankcase, as he made the rounds of the State House. He was in Augusta lobbying for passage of a mandatory book-burning act. He met with the Energy Committee to discuss "trash to energy" projects, saying "the only time this trash would do any good would be when it generated electricity for good clean homes." He met the Education Committee, where he told legislators they can't legislate immorality. When one committee member suggested that they couldn't legislate ignorance either, the Reverend said that he wasn't ignorant of the fact that some members

of the committee were probably homosexuals. His bill did not pass, and "Billy" blamed it on "those Portland homos." However, he did manage to get a resolution passed proclaiming July 17 as Intolerance Day.

I'll be in town next Wednesday for all the "hot" activities. I'll hold office hours at the Town Hall. Right now I'm holding office hours with the committee clerk over at the Senator Motel, so I'd better sign off.

POLICE BLOTTER

MONDAY 8:12 PM — Someone on Frost Avenue reported smelling a skunk. Police are still investigating.

MONDAY 10:41 PM — Two separate complaints of "snoring" on West Elm. Police are still investigating.

TUESDAY 12:19 AM — A drunk was seen relieving himself on Bill Smart's whirlygig lawn ornament. Police are still investigating.

TUESDAY 2 AM — Three elderly women were raped and murdered and their house on Fernald Road was burned to the ground. Police are still investigating.

METHODIST BEAN SUPPERS TO RETURN "TOOT SWEET"

The United Methodist Church has announced it will resume the monthly bean suppers. The supper committee announced the resumption with the terse news release: "The ventilation system has been repaired." The next supper is scheduled for Saturday.

BILL'S SUPERETTE STOCKED UP

Bill's Superette of Corsica has stocked up on matches and lighter fluid in anticipation of heavy sales next Wednesday.

IGA TRUCK

The IGA truck will unload on Thursday night this week.

88

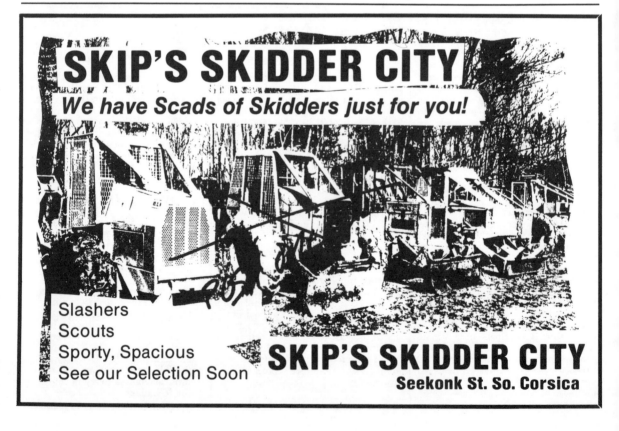

SKIP'S SKIDDER CITY
We have Scads of Skidders just for you!

Slashers
Scouts
Sporty, Spacious
See our Selection Soon

SKIP'S SKIDDER CITY
Seekonk St. So. Corsica

EDITORIAL
ISN'T OUR TOWN GREAT?

We always use this page of our paper to express the most controversial topics. With plenty of news this week, like the upcoming bonfire by the Literary Society, and the IGA truck unloading on Thursday, we sure do have plenty to voice our opinion on. So without fear of what our advertisers will say, this is our brave editorial position!

Isn't Corsica a Great Town? We just love the painted houses, the brick houses, the sidewalks and all the fine businesses that keep our town just great. If you disagree with this controversial opinion, you are free to write us. And we are free to exercise our editorial judgement and to rip up your letter. Have a nice week, you great town.

THE BIG TIME!
Town Mentioned on National TV

Corsica has hit the big time. The town was mentioned last Friday night on the TV sitcom, "Sho 'Nuff."

One of the characters, Cornbread, asked the character Frank where he got that awful hat, and Frank said, "from my dead uncle in Corsica, Maine." Cornbread replied: "He must have been dead for a long time."

After the show, the town cemetery office was flooded with calls from people around the country wanting to get red-and-black-checked woolen hats. The Chamber of Commerce is planning a Hat Day sale, and invitations have been sent to Cornbread to visit the town. No word yet on the reply.

DUFUS TO PERFORM

The noted musical comedy group Rufus Dufus and the Duffers will appear at the Corsica Grange Hall on Saturday in a benefit performance for the Collywobble Foundation. The group, which used to be great when they were on TV, will be doing their hits: "Jelly Donut," "Clam Up, Will Ya?" and the Corsica Classic: "One Night in Corsica (Is Like Two Weeks Anywhere Else)." Tickets are $5. The concert is being held despite opposition from Rev. Wilhelm "Billy" Crankcase, who has ordered his parishioners to throw all copies of Dufus's record "Skinny Dippin'" into next Wednesday's bonfire.

LIBRARY NEWS
Library Cool to Fire Plan

The Library Association elected new officers last Thursday at a meeting well attended by members of the Women's Literary Society of the Church of the Dour Redeemer. The Society managed to elect two of its members to the Library Board, including Eva Crankcase, wife of Rev. Wilhelm "Billy" Crankcase.

A lively debate was conducted on the status of the Women's Section, which had been the idea of Ima Brick, the librarian. Mrs. Crankcase suggested that the Women's Section should only contain The Total Woman and Phyllis Schlafly's Autobiography. "The rest of that trash should be thrown in the fire next Wednesday," she said, referring to books that "have women find out about things they aren't supposed to know about."

The general membership of the association resisted efforts by Mrs. Crankcase and other society members to contribute half of the library's books to the bonfire. Mrs. Crankcase did ask Librarian Brick for the key to the library, however, in order to conduct some business on Tuesday night.

FIRE DEPARTMENT NEWS

The Corsica Volunteer Fire Department had a hostile meeting with Chief Ricker Sunday afternoon. The chief wants to purchase a "safety yellow" fire truck. Members of the volunteer crew want to keep it red. The John Birch Society favors red also. One Bircher claimed the new truck would "turn America yellow and make it forget about the red problem."

The department will provide coverage for next Wednesday's bonfire at the baseball diamond. None of the volunteers plan to toss their Police Gazettes into the flames, however, the department said.

Marriages

Rhonda Varney, daughter of Mr. and Mrs. Clyde Varney Sr. of Ajax Road, to Clyde Varney, Jr., the son of Mr. and Mrs. Varney Sr. The new couple plan to make their home with their parents.

Linda Bryant, of Bucksport, to Alvin Borden of Sligo Road. Mr. Borden has been widowed six previous times, mysteriously, after his previous wives cooked a turnip dish. The new Mrs. Borden has vowed not to cook turnips.

BIRTHS

Born: To Hester Prim, who lives out on the Dump Road in the red A-frame: a daughter, whom she will name Crankcase. The father is unknown.

TV HIGHLIGHTS

Highlights from this week's programming schedule for WME-TV, all-Maine television, Corsica.

Gospel Aerobics — Start your day by lifting up your body and spirit with the "Clapping Cleric" herself, the Rev. Betty Memps and the singing "Gospel Pec Pushers."

General Delivery — Afternoon drama, produced, directed and acted by students of Corsica High School. This week, Kevin celebrates his graduation from high school a little too much and wrecks his snow machine during a mud race at the Corsica Raceway. Tammy is caught talking to a stranger.

The Wicked and the Queer — Adult drama, produced, directed and acted by the Former Student Drama Club of Corsica. This week Laurie is caught talking with a person from another town that nobody in town knows. Larry can't stop sneezing and learns a lot from an allergist. Larry Sr. leaves medical school and opens up an inn on the edge of town where an Italian count comes to stay and threatens to buy the Corsica Raceway and ban stock cars and bring in grand prix cars. Kevin is hurt in a mill accident and dies.

Corsica Magazine — With your hosts Chicky Putz and Marlene Parkins. Chicky and Marlene are on location all week at the Annual Returnable Bottle Festival. Improvements to the baselines at the Corsica Little League Field are the subject of Coach Del Viking's Sports Corner.

Luv That Vern — Flashbacks to Vern's childhood give "the missus" a few things to laugh about. Vern recalls watching *Rawhide* for the first time, then rounding up all the otters in the neighborhood for an otter drive to Skowhegan. Shows "the missus" real photos and pelts.

Smart Teen Squad — Action-packed half-hour. Members of the Corsica High School Smart Teen Club dramatize problems facing today's youth. This week Kevin pressures Candy to close her dad's store early to go bowling. Candy's mom, Candy, falls asleep while babysitting Candy and Kevin's baby, Kevin, and Kevin eats too many raisins.

The WME Event: Muskie, the Man — Chicky Putz is Edmund Muskie in this made-for-Maine TV blockbuster. This week, "the Waterville years," Muskie is fitted for a basketball uniform and his future is in doubt after a mole is removed by an incompetent dermatologist, who also unsuccessfully treats his ever-growing dandruff.

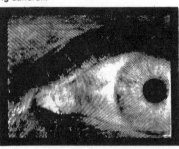

Ollie Otter says

"You otter try 'em"
"You otter buy 'em"

OTTER DOGS

Moms who want their kids to have a NATURAL taste treat serve OTTER DOGS. Made from the whole otter and nothing else.

The distinctive purple color also makes them good for arranging on the wall!

Another fine product from Velma's Kitchens. Remember, there really is a Velma!

13. CHRISTMAS, ETC.

THE TWELVE DAYS OF REAL MAINE CHRISTMAS

On the First Day of Christmas, my true love gave to me:
    A Flamingo in a Pine Tree
        (with just the cutest piece of yarn around its neck);

On the second Day of Christmas, my true love gave to me:
    Two Nasty Gansetts
        (one of 'em was already drunk);
    And a Flamingo in a Pine Tree.

On the Third Day of Christmas, my true love gave to me:
    Three Cans of Bondo
        (and a little piece of cardboard to spread it around);
    Two Nasty Gansetts;
    And a Flamingo in a Pine Tree.

On the Fourth Day of Christmas, my true love gave to me:
    Four Surplus Cheeses
        (and a little surplus cheese board and knife);
    Three Cans of Bondo;
    Two Nasty Gansetts
    And a Flamingo in a Pine Tree.

On the Fifth Day of Christmas, my true love gave to me:
    Five-Weight Chainsaw Oil
        (and the calendar that goes with it, with all them girls in bathing suits);
    Four Surplus Cheeses;
    Three Cans of Bondo;
    Two Nasty Gansetts;
    And a Flamingo in a Pine Tree.

On the Sixth Day of Christmas, my true love gave to me:
    Six Strings of Bowling
        (good for any Thursday morning in August);
    Five-Weight Chainsaw Oil;
    Four Surplus Cheeses;
    Three Cans of Bondo;
    Two Nasty Gansetts;
    And a Flamingo in a Pine Tree.

On the Seventh Day of Christmas, my true love gave to me:
    Seven Pounds of Deer Meat (from the flank section);
        (and all the other stuff mentioned on the Sixth Day).

On the Eighth Day of Christmas my true love gave to me:
    Eight Pounds of Moose Meat
        (I didn't ask where she got this);
    Seven Pounds of Deer Meat;
    Six Strings of Bowling;

92

Five-Weight Chainsaw Oil;
Four Surplus Cheeses;
Three Cans of Bondo;
Two Nasty Gansetts;
And a Flamingo in a Pine Tree.

On the Ninth Day of Christmas, my true love gave to me:
Nine Pairs of Red Flannel Underwear
(the kind you sew yourself into all winter long);
A U-Haul truck filled with all the other stuff I'd been
getting every day, including a Flamingo in a Pine Tree.

On the Tenth Day of Christmas, my true love gave to me:
Ten Packs of Generic Cigarettes
(in a nice carton marked "Butts");
Nine Pairs Red Underwear;
Eight Pounds Moose Meat;
Seven Pounds Deer Meat;
Six Strings Bowling;
Five-Weight Chainsaw Oil;
Four Surplus Cheeses;
Three Cans Bondo;
Two Nasty Gansetts;
Flamingo-Pine Tree.

On the Eleventh Day of Christmas, my true love gave to me:
An Eleven-Month Subscription to *Trailer Life*
(she bought it from the newsboy, who's putting himself through oil-burner school);
Plus, what looked like a "Yard Sale in a Box," until I figured
it was all the stuff I had been getting all along, including
that darn Flamingo in the Pine Tree.

On the Twelfth Day of Christmas my true love gave to me:
One Dozen Assorted Bumper Stickers with right-wing slogans on them
like "Nuclear Power Plants Are Built Better Than Jane Fonda";
Eleven-Month Subscription to *Trailer Life*;
Ten Packs of Butts;
Nine More Longjohns;
Eight Pounds Viande de Mousse;
Seven Pounds Venison;
Six Strings of Bowling;
Five-Weight Chainsaw Oil;
Four Surplus Cheeses;
Three Cans of Bondo;
Two Nasty Gansetts;
And a Flamingo in a Pine Tree.

On the Thirteenth Day of Christmas my true love said to me: "What are you going to do with all this culch around here? You wonder why you can never find anything, it's because you got junk everywhere. What are we gonna do with all that Bondo? You'd better do something with that deer meat. It's beginning to smell wicked. I wish the hell you'd pick up your empty beer cans. And don't you think it's time we took the Christmas tree down? All the needles fell on the floor a week ago."

SCRATCH 'N' SMELL

There are so many ways to capture the essence of Maine. People have always had a visual association — such as the lighthouses painted on black velvet or the quaint postcards of small Maine towns. The sounds of Maine are available, of course, through such Maine institutions as Wicked Good Band records. And there has always been a taste image associated with foods such as lobster, blueberries, and Italian sandwiches. Now, for the first time, we are pleased to present the odors of Maine, available either in Scratch 'n' Smell cards or in Maine Spray Smells aerosol cans. Our scientists have worked wonders to recreate the smorgasbord of olfactory stimulation that is Maine.

Give one of the tastefully colored cards a scratch, or just touch the nozzle on the decorator cans. Here's what you might come up with:

Salt-sea air, old lobster pots, and just a touch of clambake in the distance. When you get this scent, you've got the **Maine Seacoast** at its finest. A traditional classic.

Pizza, motor oil, suntan lotion, and well-done Canadienne sandals. All these scents are in **Old Orchard Beach**. You can go there by way of your nose, without all the hassle of the parking and the strange tourists.

Pine trees, mountain air, budworm spray and moose droppings. All in one great scent: **The Maine Woods**. You can actually be in the woods without all the black flies, the sudden thunderstorms, the gaunt people.

Quiche, Chanel #5, and the exhaust fumes from a 1985 dark-green Volvo station wagon. Everybody becomes a young professional when they sniff the historic and trendy **Old Port District** of Portland.

Of course, each set contains a surprise as well. These are great as conversation starters, or as hostess gifts.

"Why, what's this?" your hostess will ask.

"It's a surprise. Just scratch 'n' sniff," you say.

She scratches. She sniffs. "Lord, who cut the cheese?"

Oops, you've just been surprised by **Evening in Westbrook** — so realistic you'd think you were underneath a paper mill.

Scratch 'n' Smell cards and Maine Spray Smells are great for collecting — and for trading.

"Say, Hiram, I see you've got an extra of the **Litchfield Fair.** I'll trade you one of my extra **L.L. Bean Trout Pond** cards."

"I don't know, Ephraim, I'm kinda partial to the **Litchfield Fair.** How about the inside left pant leg of **Miss Maine's Snowsuit?**"

From the musty confines of a country museum to the musky madness of the Maine Mariners locker room...from the sharp bite of a bait shed to the pungent pleasure of a bean supper, it's Maine Spray Smells or Scratch 'n' Smell cards!

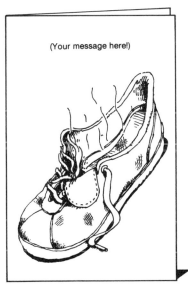

(Your message here!)

Dubberware Miracle Sox

How many times have you heard someone say this: "If they can put a trout pond in the middle of L.L. Bean's store, why can't they do something about keeping socks fresh and clean smelling?" Now, with Dubberware's Miracle Sox, you can!

Over the years, you've come to depend on Dubberware and the patented Belching Lid System to keep your food fresh. Now the same engineers who brought you the Belching Lid System for food bring it to your feet! No more sweaty socks! No more embarassing foot odor! Just clean, fresh socks and feet — all the time!

Here's how they work: choose the Miracle Sox that are right for you — they come in most shoe sizes and widths and many popular styles. Put your feet in the comfortable contours of your Miracle Sox and squeeze them 'til they belch. Belching locks in freshness and locks out sweat and odor. All day long, you won't know they're on, they're that comfortable! Then at the end of the day, take them off, wipe with a damp sponge, and they're ready to wear the next day.

Dubberware Miracle Sox have revolutionized footwear, but they're not sold in every store. They're available only at Dubberware Parties. And when you're at the next Dubberware Party, ask your Dubberware Lady about Dubbydipes, Dubberware's new reusable diapers, and Dubbeats, edible Dubberware for those office parties when nobody wants to clean up. Dubbeats come in several flavors!

WICKED GOOD

(SPOKEN) Dear Velma, Sorry to hear you had to go to prison for shooting seagulls. I wanted you to know my heart still beats for you. I've been missin' you something wicked. I know the warden lets you listen to tape recordings. So me and the boys went down to Old Orchard Beach. We each put a quarter in the recording booth, and we came up with this song — just for you...

WICKED GOOD. I love ya darlin' 'cause you're Wicked Good.
You started fires in my heart of wood,
And they're burnin' hot because you're Wicked Good.

Wicked Sharp. Everything about you is Wicked Sharp.
When I saw you at the counter of the old K-Mart
I fell in love with you because you're Wicked Sharp.

I've been halfway 'round the world and halfway back again,
From Paris, Maine, to Paris, France.
And you're the cutest girl I ever have seen.
Won't you take me to the dance?

Wicked Good. Our life together will be Wicked Good.
Even when our teeth fall out it's understood
They'll be chattering away: you're Wicked Good.

(Spoken) "Well, Fred, where did you ever find such a cunnin' girl?
  "I told ya, t'was at the K-Mart, she was a blue-light special for a buck, 2.98."
  "She always looked kinda massive to me."
  "No, she ain't massive. That's just from the front. You turn her sideways,
  step back a couple steps — she looks wicked decent."

I've been halfway 'round the world and halfway back again.
From Paris, Maine, to Paris, France.
And you're the most cunnin' girl I ever did see.
I think I'm gonna wet my pants.

Darlin', Wicked Good. And our romance too, it's Wicked Good.
And just like turnips you're my favorite food —
Breakfast, lunch and dinner, Wicked Good.

Mm-mm...Wicked Good!

Christmas in Maine: no credit.